ARLINGTON'S BLOOD

ARLINGTON'S BLOOD

Written by AN AMERICAN

iUniverse, Inc.

New York Lincoln Shanghai

ARLINGTON'S BLOOD

iUniverse, Inc.

For information address:
iUniverse, Inc.
2021 Pine Lake Road, Suite 100
Lincoln, NE 68512
www.iuniverse.com

ISBN: 0-595-32332-4

Printed in the United States of America

Contents

THE PERPETUAL PROJECT

Some projects never seem to end. The "cold Tuesday in January" in the first sentence of the **ARLINGTON'S BLOOD** chapter was when I was in Washington for the Clinton inauguration in 1993 as one among the masses. I had started developing these thoughts almost a decade before, while recuperating from a bone marrow transplant in Seattle in 1984. Long periods of lying flat on one's back, especially when a month of the time is in the sterile seclusion of a "bubble" environment, gives an opportunity to think that most people never have the privilege of. But I did not know how to organize the thoughts until that trip to Washington, where I also pondered the small block of granite that was the original D.C. memorial for Franklin Roosevelt. It occurred to me then that I could organize them along an outline of FDR's "Four Freedoms," of Speech and Religion, and from Want and Fear. It was not until two years later, during 1995, that I started refining my notes into prose.

I first entitled the work to follow on the outline, **Liberty and Law (Finding Balance in the Four Freedoms)**, and set about to find a publisher under my own name. Even though I was not well known, I hoped that the fact that I had earned a law degree after a life threatening illness might at least get some small publishing outfit or agent to give it a serious look, but not so. The least courteous of the rejections that I received upon sending out twenty or so inquiries with copies of my little book asked, "Who in the hell are you?" So, I thought I was laying the project to rest on the night before my wedding in October 1995, when I took all but one of the remaining copies and had a mock book signing, giving them out to my friends and brothers between beers and laughs about it being soon after Colin Powell set book signing volume records for his autobiography. And I did lay it to rest. After doing some editing in 1996 to try to keep it current for the sake of my own thought processes, I even scrapped making that effort on a consistent basis.

I don't remember looking at it again to any extent until after I mentioned it as a major life project while taking a self-inventory course at my church in late 2001. I re-read it thoroughly then and recognized that, aside from some adjustments for money over time, most of the work was as current in 2001 as when I had first put it together in 1995.

I also heard about iUniverse at around the same time and thought of giving that mode of publication a try. But I had also gone through a harrowing job misadventure during 2000-2001. Defying this experience by making an unusual educational achievement, just as I had with my sickness, was the most positive way that I could think of to cope with it. So, the project went back on the shelf while the months of August 2002 through May 2004 were dominated by the rigors of an MBA Program as I continued to work full-time as an attorney. But, I did manage to renew the editing process toward a revived goal of getting it into print.

Considering the lack of acceptance by publishers and agents for the first effort, I decided not to use my own name this time. It is true that I am blessed to be well educated, with a bachelor's degree, a law degree and an MBA from three of our nation's fine universities. I say blessed because a person like me, raised with four younger siblings by our mother, would have been lucky in years gone past to even be literate, even in America.

Yet, my practice of law for more than a decade has not been high profile. The one extraordinary legal struggle that I was involved in so far was not accorded significant media attention, at least not the type and degree of attention that I thought it deserved. And, although I now have an MBA, I expect to remain a lawyer and have no record or intention of running a company. But, the fact is that my credentials would have been the same had I been the most famous and skilled lawyer alive or had run a Fortune 500 company, or had I lived and undertaken this project in a past age when I could not have gained my education. For my only authority would still be that of a citizen, authorized and entitled by birth to offer an opinion, albeit a relatively well informed one. The basic concept of the project has always been that notoriety and years of policy shaping experience are not prerequisites for a citizen to respectfully propose alternatives, and explain the reasoning behind them. So, public identification of the work with me is unimportant. Though the opinions are offered as respectfully as I have been able to manage, some of them may not seem in vogue for how some of my fellow citizens of the United States of America may define patriotism in 2004. Therefore, I thought it fitting to declare my allegiance in the nom de plume.

ARLINGTON'S BLOOD

Alone in our nation's capital on a cold Tuesday in January, I decided to visit an attraction previously missed, the National Cemetery at Arlington. The subway ride with other tourists to the front gate of the famous graveyard provided no hint of the healing, and the wounding, that I would experience there.

The healing came quickly. My shoulders sagged under a burden of sadness when I arrived in the capital the day before. Walking with groups of school children in respect and quiet among the thousands of reminders of those who had given their lives to continue this American democracy brought the problems of my life into better focus. The cure of perspective was accepted with an embarrassed smile.

But the cure for an ailing heart opened the door for a great wounding of my soul. For walking closer to the markers allowed each tree to stand forth boldly from the former anonymity of the forest.

A few provided memorials to the famous—John and Robert Kennedy, boxing champion Joe Louis, and those who died in the Challenger space shuttle disaster among them. But the vast majority were there to remind of little known soldiers from all states and of all races and faiths.

Arrival at the Tomb of the Unknown Soldier, the memorial set forth for all whose identities are "known only to God," accompanied by the mournful sound of the afternoon taps, led me to ask what messages the unknown hosts would send to the living. What would these who had served in danger and lost their lives say—not to the families and friends left behind, but to me and those by my side on that blustery day, unknown and unimagined, who have just as surely gained from their sacrifices as if we had been friends or relatives?

The answer returned in the silence of my imagination with the emotional force of a cannon's report. It came from the graves of black and white, rich and poor, farmer and city dweller, immigrant and native born. It rang as loudly from the graves of atheists as it did from those of the faithful. The voice of the blood of the sharecropper united with that of the landowner. The blood of Arlington seemed to cry out in my mind that day, "This mission must not fail!" And hearing the voice of that blood delivered the wound, which was to understand that it could fail.

The United States of America represents the greatest democratic experiment the world will ever know. We cannot presume that such a collection of courage and genius will ever again be united in one cause as was the case during our revolution and the creation of our republic. Nor is it likely, with the advent of mass communications and modern weaponry and surveillance, that such a group could perform its work in the type of security and privacy necessary for accomplishment of the task, even if one could again be assembled.

No, it will never happen again. But the grand mission launched by our nation's founders now stands in jeopardy. Crime and terror color the simplest decisions of our people, from allowing the children out to play, to taking a walk to the corner store or making a business flight to an American city.

Debt overburdens our government. Millions of willing workers are denied a livable day's wage for an honest day's toil. Many with jobs are frustrated and exhausted by unyielding demands to do more with less as they watch some business profits and executive salaries, and the percentage of national wealth controlled by relatively fewer people, climb ever higher.

Extremes of religion and anti-religion intimidate, dominate and subjugate the actions and minds of the majority. Other extremists promote violence, vulgarity and privacy invasion, or bind up creativity and learning, in perversion of the precious freedoms of speech and religion.

The self-discipline and courage of our citizens, and the public and private actions resulting from those unseen powers, have always been our only defenses against societal imbalance and eventual collapse or tyranny. As we have borne the burdens of establishing and preserving the world's freedoms in recent decades, we seem to have become weary as we have continued to bear our own. Yet, as we consider our past and envision the future, we can create new energy for reshaping our present.

As an energetic new focus on the present develops, we can better understand the future, realizing that the cost of failure of the true "American dream," that we can effectively govern ourselves, is far too high to pay. For the importance of this nation and its continuation far exceed the worth of our own lives or those of our children. All the blood of Arlington poured forth from someone's child.

Our thinking will then be expanded to comprehend what is really at stake. It is a future world without a shining beacon to light the path for others. It is a future world doomed to plunge into a new dark age in which the freedoms of man descend to the status of myth.

We have wisely chosen to reject the false idea of a royal line by which to pre-serve our society. It falls upon the citizens of each generation to pass an effective democracy on to the next. Our destiny's time is now.

It is not enough for this present generation to seek to restore past glories with shines already dimmed under the harsh light of unvarnished history. We will seize the idea of a future greater than our past when we allow the greatness within us to speak, a greatness shown by our distinct heritage, diverse yet united unlike any other in the history of humankind.

In doing so, we will defy the walls of frustration that confront us, and we will learn that they must fall to the power of our united hope; hope that is not a con-venient sedative but an aggressive and unyielding force. Only then will we earn the honor of a look beyond those walls. What will we see?

We will see a nation without fear of damage to our persons or property from crime. We will have no fear of law-breaker or law enforcer because justice will be fair and swift.

We will see a nation where all who are willing and able to work have jobs by which they can support themselves and their families. It will also be a nation where those able but not willing to work receive nothing in return for nothing, because it is a nation of equity. It will be a nation where no citizen is denied an opportunity to obtain appropriate medical care, and where all who benefit from a quality health care system share fairly in the responsibility of maintaining it.

We will see a nation where the rights of all to practice their religions are pro-tected by the people, but where no religion is coerced upon the people. It will be a nation that honors its religious heritage by allowing its citizens to exercise choice in the same way that the Almighty permitted the denizens of Eden to choose.

It will be a nation that recognizes men and women as equal partners in its suc-cess. And it will be a nation where people of all races are recognized for the equal worth of their equal humanity.

We will see a nation that hates war. It will seek to lead by the example of goodness, but will fight with full fury when it must.

President Franklin D. Roosevelt outlined the mission for such a nation in an address to Congress in January 1941. He stated that we seek to secure a world founded upon "four essential human freedoms," freedom of speech, freedom of religion, freedom from want and freedom from fear.

FREEDOM OF SPEECH

This freedom is the foundation for the other three. Freedom of religion would be empty without the right to openly communicate to God and to other people about God. Freedom from want depends on receiving messages concerning opportunities and objects that we need or desire and our ability to freely accept or reject those offers. Freedom from fear depends on receiving messages of warning or relief from that which threatens us, as well as our ability to confidently and securely communicate to seek assistance from others or means to protect ourselves.

Speech is hard to define. It includes the spoken and written word, as well as silent prayers whispered in the closets of our souls. Many symbols and acts are also speech. Hand gestures can speak volumes. The hearing and speech impaired have a system of language uttered by the hands with no sounds. The sight-impaired have raised Braille symbols to which sensitive fingers ascribe meaning. A dance can convey emotions that words cannot express.

The context in which speech is conveyed, such as at what volume or by what means it is delivered, can sometimes be regulated. For instance, we are fully entitled to use the tool of government to set limits on late night speeches in residential neighborhoods, or on the broadcast of pornography over the public property of the airwaves.

Nevertheless, the roots of speech in the mind and soul make external regulation of even its delivery context difficult. The actual content of the messages, on the other hand, can only be effectively regulated by individual self-discipline, as dictated by self-interest.

1. The Vote As Speech

Speech reaches the height of its strength in the silence of the voting booth. Only death is a greater equalizer than the vote, the primary unifying principle of democracy. It is gratifying to see the nation's candidates for President exit the voting booths on Election Day. After all the speeches, debates, charges and counter-charges go silent, they have only the power of a citizen to cast a vote according to conscience.

It is a tribute to the greatness of our nation's people that we accept those who are elected as entitled to their terms, and that the previously elected step aside when they are rejected. All nations do not transfer power with such civility.

The vote represents raw power. To begin to understand and appreciate the power and the privilege of our right to vote is to tap into the eternal power of choice and free conscience. It is a high responsibility and duty that Arlington's blood implores us to take. Memorial Day celebrations, wreaths and remembrances ring hollow if we do not pay the appropriate first tribute to the fallen. Those who lived and died to create and preserve the right to vote are honored best when the following generations exercise that right.

The question is not whether we should or should not vote. We must vote for the nation to continue in a form that seeks to preserve and strengthen experience of the four freedoms.

The question is how we should vote. Not how, as in which competing alternatives to choose. But how in a broader sense, as in with what information, good or bad, accurate or false, our voting decisions are formed.

2. Broadcast Campaigning and Fairness

Limitation of Access

We should carefully consider mass broadcasting technology's ability to shape voting decisions. Newspapers and magazines may be biased toward the political left or right. But the option always remains for those of opposing views to get messages out in print. Handbills can be used to cover large areas in a short time with relatively little expense. And the Internet has now multiplied that potential.

The general public cannot duplicate a mass produced newspaper's influence. But, specific positions put forth in it can be effectively countered by use of the print medium. The success of petition drives opposing positions advanced by mass publications proves this point. Thus, while difficult, it is economically practicable to answer print with print.

The same is not nearly so true of the broadcast media. The number of available broadcast frequencies has increased, but the increase in the number of frequencies accorded credibility by the public has not nearly kept pace with the number of people desiring to speak by broadcast. Thus, while an area may have many more operating radio and television frequencies and channels than newspapers, the meaningful use of broadcast is subject to a much lower rate of public access than the print medium.

This factor has contributed to an increased price of access, shown by the astronomical growth in costs for advertising during televised major events, such as Super Bowls or last episodes of popular programs, and for running credible political campaigns. The increased demand and resulting increases in pricing have caused a decrease in meaningful access to the broadcast frequencies. The opportunity for an effective response by the same broadcast medium usually only exists for the very wealthy or those whom the wealthy choose to finance.

Additionally, only one person or group can effectively deliver a message on a given channel at a given time. As argument format news programs show, we can only understand one shouted message at a time. Unless you can gain access to a channel that is already widely viewed or listened to, there is little practical hope that you can widely disseminate your message in a reasonably prompt manner. Consequently, public access cable television channels are not an adequate remedy.

The print medium, on the other hand, only has an access threshold of affording paper, ink and a means to copy. While we can still only read one of many available print messages at a time, the preservation of different messages in print allows us to save them for reading at a later time much more readily than for recorded messages. Competing arguments shouted at the same time over a recorded broadcast will be just as muddled the second, third or fourth times that we replay them as they were the first time.

Thus, the print medium fosters a more true degree of competition among ideas. It places emphasis upon the priorities and time management of the customers, the intended receivers of the messages, rather than on the messenger with the loudest voice, whether the loudness results from powerful lungs, notoriety or means by which to monopolize broadcast time.

Limitation of access is an inherent characteristic of the broadcast media that cannot be corrected. This unchangeable feature allows electronic merchants of style over substance who can gain meaningful broadcast media access, which goes to the highest bidder, to use inflammatory topics of the day to sway voters by emotion rather than reasoned thought. And this is done with the tool of the public property of the airwaves.

Sloganism

We have all seen and heard examples of a person or party repeating slogans, with a background of waving flags and stirring music, without giving any suggestion of what ideas are proposed to implement the supposed bases of the slogans. It is safe to assume that there is no credible idea when one is not openly proposed. The slogan thus becomes the end, rather than the means to an end.

Slogans have long played a key part in American political life. Andrew Jackson served two terms as President as "the hero of New Orleans." President William Henry Harrison also used a slogan, "Tippecanoe and Tyler, too," to transfer battlefield success to the political arena.

Public policy issues have been similarly summarized in slogans to move the people. The debate over the line of latitude that would mark the northwest boundary between the United States and Canada was framed in terms of "Fifty-four forty or fight!"

All of these slogans, used to abbreviate issues and add entertainment value to campaigns, were prominent well before we learned to broadcast messages over the airwaves. However, they were also used during a time when skills in writing and speaking were the main tools of persuasion, when two-hour political speeches and sustained debates, such as those between Abraham Lincoln and Stephan Douglas, were primary sources of entertainment and enlightenment.

The proven effectiveness of broadcast advertising technology has combined with the inherent limitation of meaningful access to create a broadcast media system in which the vast majority of modern political energy and spending goes toward marketing slogans. When the political system revolves almost completely around sloganism, with few resources remaining for emphasizing careful consideration of real solutions to real problems, the system has become unbalanced. This unbalanced and unhealthy state is where the American political system now stands.

Public Property

It is important to remember that the broadcast frequencies have long been considered public property in this nation. This is the basis for government licensing of the use of those frequencies.

Government licensing and regulation of use of the public property of the airwaves is different than would be licensing or regulation of the private property of a printing press or the public expression of the private thoughts of a speaker or writer. The broadcast frequencies are more like our national parklands, treasures held in trust for the benefit of all citizens. As citizens, we are entitled to regulate use of such jointly owned resources through our government.

Reasonable people do not doubt the right of the citizenry to corporately license a driver's right to operate on the public highways. We do so to require that conduct must be responsible when it is granted relevance by the use of public property. Similarly, a television or radio frequency license is designed to require responsible broadcasting. This right of the citizenry to regulate the use of our airwaves has been supported by numerous Supreme Court majority opinions over the years.

Some suggest that broadcasters be allowed to buy the frequencies for operation as private property. Raising money for the government, and broadcasters' complaints of coerced "self-censorship," are offered as the justifications.

This idea should be rejected. Selling off the right of the people to legally require responsible broadcasting will compromise the potential for legal control over political campaign spending and broadcast pornography and indecency.

One of our society's foundational beliefs is that free speech is one of our greatest tools for progress. We believe that if we protect the rights of all to speak and communicate, the most productive and beneficial ideas will eventually prevail.

This optimistic creed has proven true for us many times as we have sailed the perilous sea of Nationhood for more than two centuries. Thus, there is now no credible question under the law that the speaker's right to express is the primary object of the Constitution's protection of non-broadcast speech, the only kind that existed when the document was written.

The Preamble to our Constitution states that the document was written "to form a more perfect Union, establish justice, insure domestic tranquility, provide for the common defense, promote the general welfare, and secure the blessings of liberty to ourselves and our posterity...." All that follows in the document is within the context of helping bring the goals in the Preamble to pass. Therefore, all of the rights recognized in the document, including the right of free speech, are means to an end, our tools for building "a more perfect Union."

Placing the right of the people to receive fair and accurate broadcast speech messages over the right of the broadcaster to speak meets the constitutional Preamble test. Broadcast speech cannot be used as a tool by the general American public to build "a more perfect Union" if it can be monopolized with impunity by particular vested financial or governmental interests.

Limitation of access justifies different standards of constitutional protection associated with the right of a person or association to speak over the airwaves and the right of the same person or group to communicate by non-broadcast means. Access to public forums, such as the streets and parks, is widely available for all of our non-broadcast messages. But access is extremely limited for the would-be broadcast speaker.

The dilemma of the physical impossibility of creating meaningfully widespread access to the broadcast frequencies has made the two-sided coin of differing constitutional rights associated with non-broadcast and broadcast speech necessary. While it is the right of the speaker that prevails in non-broadcast speech, it must be the right of the people to receive balanced information, not the right of the broadcaster to express views, which is the primary consideration when use of the public property of the airwaves is at issue. Or, as the Supreme Court has stated, it is the right of the people to receive balanced information that is "paramount" in the area of broadcast speech.

Placing the emphasis of broadcast speech rights on the side of broadcasters' rights to speak will result in the kind of thought and behavior control that we have learned of in other nations whose unfortunate peoples are fed a steady stream of broadcast propaganda. This condition has sadly increased in our own land as we have become complacent in maintaining the proper balance of broadcast speech rights.

However, so long as the citizenry maintains final control of our government through the vote and public ownership of the airwaves, we have the power to demand that some degree of responsibility and fairness will be exercised by those granted license to use our property. The emphasis of broadcast speech rights protection must rest with the listeners, the message receivers, to keep free speech from being perverted into a tool of destruction rather than building. Only continuing public ownership can provide a continuing legal justification for maintaining the emphasis on the side of the majority.

There has been a marked increase in use of the airwaves for transparent political purposes under the guise of providing news or other services since the repeal of the "fairness doctrine" in the late 1980s. This doctrine, in existence in some form for most of the last century, required broadcasters who expressed opinions on political matters to grant free access to the airwaves for opposing viewpoints in limited circumstances. It treated personal character attacks by broadcasters in the same manner: not by taking away the right to attack, but by providing the attacked person time to respond over the same medium. Some who wished to use the people's airwaves without restraint for purposes of propaganda and profit denounced the doctrine, branding it as a law that required self-censorship.

The fact is that the law was only rarely enforced. The scarcity of enforcement resulted from the scarcity of editorializing and the infrequent personal character assassination engaged in by broadcasters while the law was on the books.

But, placing the right of the people to receive unbiased information over broadcast rights of expression and profit making was resented. The resentment stemmed from the imposition of self-discipline upon the users of public property by the citizen owners of that property rather than from "self-censorship," which is merely a deceptive slogan. The attitude of a camper in a national forest claiming to be oppressed because of laws against littering the campground would be the same.

We should carefully consider the results of eliminating the responsibility previously generated by the fairness doctrine from the privilege of using our valuable public property. And we should ask ourselves whether the quality and tone of discussion of issues in our country have improved since removal of this restraint.

Personal attacks by broadcast have greatly increased since the fairness doctrine's demise. Competition from the irresponsible has led formerly honorable and relatively dependable news broadcasters to descend into speculation on unfounded charges. This has caused unjustified destruction of the reputations of private citizens as well as public officials, and a resulting decrease in the people's trust in those elected and appointed to operate their state and federal governments.

Entire programs have been broadcast with the sole purpose of the character assassination of those with whom the financiers of the programs disagree. Even some religious broadcasters, who formerly used their airtime to lead people to a higher and better life, succumbed to the temptation of practicing the premise that the end justifies the means.

Even if the truth is revealed at a later date, the damage has usually been done, with images of deception ingrained in the people's minds, and another blow delivered to democracy. One of the greatest services that could be performed to begin to rid unjustified cynicism from the minds of the people, and to restore our sense of civic pride, would be to enact a new fairness doctrine patterned after the one that worked so well for so long.

Campaign Reform

Individual and group contributions of money to political campaigns are legally limited under a rationale that the contributors' political speech rights are only being indirectly restrained. However, there is little justifiable basis for limiting the amount of money that can be spent by an individual candidate for ethical, non-broadcast, purposes.

But it is entirely reasonable and legal to limit the capacity of an individual or group for renting publicly owned property, space on our airwaves, for political purposes. For it is the rights of the listeners, not the speakers, that prevail when the public property of the airwaves is in use.

A better way of allocating use of the people's airwaves for political purposes would be to limit the amount of set broadcast time that could be bought by parties, candidates or associations on a sliding scale based on a credible showing of public support, with no party or association ever entitled to more than one-half of the time made available. Present conditions, with no more than one-third of the population identifying strongly with either of the two major parties, would allow broadcast parity for a unifying third party. The major parties would be forced to reflect public desires and dreams or drift into history, endorsing our historical American mandate toward competition.

Reducing campaign media expenses would lower the threshold of money raising requirements, increasing the field of potential candidates. Requiring candidates to provide dependable evidence of threshold public support by means such as party affiliation records, legitimate polls or petitions would prevent over-fragmentation of the allotted airtime.

By thus pushing the emphasis of political campaigns away from broadcast purchasing, we would reduce the focus on sloganism, force an emphasis on organization and volunteer participation and increase the likelihood of a legitimate debate on relevant issues. Political parties, and the candidates rising through their ranks, would gain or lose support based upon more accurate assessments of the ideas that they promote.

Perhaps most importantly, such changes would reduce the opportunity for well-financed persons or vested interests to influence elections and votes of Congress beyond the level at which their views find support among the public. Our elections, in which the adult citizenry is already free to vote, would thereby also become fairer.

We should not be satisfied until the civic duties of voting and educating ourselves for it become so frequently practiced by such a large majority of the citizenry that there can be no credible doubt that those elected have strong authority to act according to their views of the public interest. Obstructionists will continue to be able to hinder public progress until we reach this goal.

The goal cannot be reached so long as political campaigning continues to be dominated by broadcast slogans. And the emphasis on sloganism will certainly continue until the people demand a return to responsible use of the public property of our airwaves.

The Supreme Court's decision to uphold the McCain-Feingold campaign reform bill's limits on "soft money" to political parties and on broadcast attack ads in the waning days of campaigns provided steps in the right direction. But, we still badly need a new fairness doctrine.

3. Entertainment and the Arts

Public ownership of the airwaves also endorses our corporate right to monitor the civility of broadcast entertainment. Entertainers and broadcasters have no standing to tell citizens to "just turn it off." But the citizenry does have the standing, right and responsibility to tell the broadcasters to.

Neither the government nor the telephone companies encourage us to "just hang up" on obscene callers whose offensive messages are delivered into our homes over privately owned phone lines. Rather, there are penalties upon identification of the culprits. We are likely to eventually move toward similar legal conclusions about unsolicited computer messages. Nearly everyone (except the culprits) finds such rules reasonable.

It makes no sense to limit the rights of obscene callers or computer spammers to use almost universally accessible private property more than we limit broadcasters' licensed use of very limited access public property. Studies will never be able to definitively show a link between broadcast bad behavior and imitative acting out on the part of those who receive the messages. Even so, we should err on the side of restraint when we are dealing with the potential impact of using a public commodity, the airwaves, on peoples' lives.

Regulation through elected government precludes a takeover of our airwaves by those whom most of us may consider to be hyper-moral. The great majority of the people do not glorify rape or other acts of sadism, nor do we tend to hurl unprovoked vulgarities at or show nude bodies to strangers. We have a corporate right to seek and reach agreement on imposing reasonable restraints on broadcasters who profit by being granted the privilege of using our public property.

That corporate right lessens with respect to specifically paid for entertainment, such as obtained through premium cable channels, even when they are transmitted over the airwaves. The corporate regulation right is very limited with respect to movies and recordings for which people pay to see or listen to in theatres or the privacy of their homes, where public property is not involved.

The public ownership rationale applicable to the airwaves is also relevant to public funding of the arts. The freedom of the artist to express is not conjoined with a right to receive public support for the expression.

Works of art and broadcasts which can reasonably be expected to be offensive to a significant number of citizens, such as those involving desecration of symbols of religion, ethnicity or patriotism, should not be publicly funded. The mistake of allowing such funding in a few highly publicized cases has provided anecdotal evidence that has been used by some in efforts toward terminating all public funding of the arts and broadcasting.

Termination of public funding for entertainment and the arts will hurt average rural Americans much more than city dwellers. Those in the cities will continue to have ready access to a broad range of artistic expression due to increased availability of private and business sources of funding.

However, many small towns, particularly those located at considerable distances from major cities, may no longer be able to support a symphony or local theatre without public funding of the arts. They may also lose access to public broadcasting radio and television channels that are not driven by the quest for profit.

The populations of our small towns will be deprived of enjoying a large part of the spectrum of wholesome American culture and education by elimination of public funding. Furthermore, necessary doctors, lawyers and other professionals will have to be paid more to live and work in the small towns without the additional quality of life provided by such cultural outlets.

The increased costs for professional services will be borne by all those needing them in the community. Thus, the efforts to discontinue public funding of the arts and broadcasting should be rejected as detrimental to the cultural and financial health of millions of our nation's families.

4. Hate Speech

On April 19, 1995, terrorists bombed our Federal Building in Oklahoma City, Oklahoma, murdering dozens of adults and children and causing millions of dollars of damage to our national property. Most of our nation was emotionally shaken by this incident.

The media focus on the crime included speculations that the perpetrators may have been motivated by propagandistic broadcasts, speeches and writings of demagogues. Similar speculations have been made concerning the murders of abortion providers.

What we should always remember about demagogues is that their primary motivation is usually money. What they really want most of the time is a contribution or sale or endorsement. They are typically entertainers with very little real intention of disrupting the status quo since that would probably cause them to lose money. It is their gullible followers that mistake the harangues of the carnival barker for the impassioned pleas of the patriot or prophet, and who always commit the aggressive acts. Implementation of a new fairness doctrine for broadcasters would put most such charlatans out of business, saving the hard-earned money of the gullible and reducing the chances for our country to experience the occasional violent acting out of the misled.

We should not, however, be tempted to try to further regulate inflammatory speech that does not make use of the public property of the broadcast frequencies. The laws are sufficient as they stand to punish irresponsible speech outside of this context. Our First Amendment is designed to protect the unpopular and seemingly unreasonable, both in faith that truth eventually will prevail and in acknowledgement that today's popular opinion may well be proven as tomorrow's error.

5. Flag Burning

Recurring proposals to amend our Constitution to prevent burning of our nation's flag manifest the folly of attempting to regulate both speech content and context. Some obsessed with numerous constitutional amendments remind me of the person who laid his hammer to the Michelangelo statue of David several years ago. His actions begged the question of whether he actually thought he could improve upon the masterpiece or hated it because it was beyond his ability to comprehend.

Burning our nation's flag in an act of disrespect is hated by most of us. But the same act becomes a solemn occasion of reflection, which delivers a message of pride and patriotism, when the local Boy Scout troop disposes of worn flags in the legally prescribed manner, by burning.

Thus, the attempt to restrain the burning of our flag by constitutional amendment is based on policing thoughts, the motives behind the burnings. Motive is a key element of prosecutions for criminal acts, such as murder. However, a constitutionally authorized incursion of the government into the mind relative to flag burning is needless when the law already forbids burning others' property.

It is hard to imagine an intended legal doctrine that is more opposed to the foundational pillar of American freedom of speech: that we are free to disagree with one another. Furthermore, the implementation of such a misguided amendment to the Constitution would likely unleash a rash of rebellious flag burnings, creating a result entirely inconsistent with the intent of the proposed amendment. Our leaders should lay aside such emotionalism and seek to guide the energy of our people toward resolving problems that are more readily measured by objective bases, such as crime and budget deficits.

FREEDOM OF RELIGION

E Pluribus Unum—it is a Latin phrase printed on our dollar bill and appearing on our national seal. It means "out of many, one." The national motto was changed in the early 1950s from "E Pluribus Unum" to "In God We Trust." Even so, Americans who do not trust or believe in God are no less (or more) entitled to the benefits and responsibilities of American life than any other citizens. The blood of those who did not trust in God is mingled with that of those who did at Arlington. Therefore, E Pluribus Unum, the idea of creating unity out of diversity, must remain a central tenet of American life.

It is especially true that during the times of stress or crisis upon which we most often expect domestic policy to focus, such as when our physical or financial health has been threatened, the faithful are most likely to seek comfort and direction from religion. Thus, the practical responsibilities of government are seldom far removed from the impulses of the people toward the divine. Nevertheless, it is difficult to imagine a more offensive domestic policy than would be the case if government should attempt to dictate to us what form of religion we may participate in when, or if, we choose to participate.

1. Religion and Government

By considering the collapse of the Soviet Communist system, we can get an idea of how reprehensible, and vain, it is for government to attempt to outlaw religion. The peoples' minds are stifled and their creativity limited when they are taught not to look beyond their individual lives and their impact upon the state.

It is just as reprehensible for human government to be united with religion, any religion, as it is for it to try to ban or discredit religion. Many of us pray for a day when some of the more religiously dogmatic among us will acknowledge that they are only interpreting the scriptures of their particular faiths to the best of their abilities, rather than passing on the definitive edicts of the Almighty.

Much controversy and ill will over questions which the human mind and experience cannot provide definite answers to will be eliminated if that occurs. However, such an acknowledgement will likely be a long time coming, for it will

18

also result in at least a tacit admission by some people with purely financial or political motives that they have been using the holy faiths of the good hearted to whip up frenzies of emotion over issues having questionable religious bases and even less legitimate political bases.

One of the foundational motivations for the Protestant Reformation in sixteenth century Europe was a belief that the church laity is entitled to read the scriptures and make their own efforts at good faith interpretation aside from the dogmas issued by the church leadership. Some of the following represents my efforts, offered in a spirit of readily acknowledged fallibility, to show that people of good faith can arrive at different conclusions on important religious matters.

The Bible and the Constitution

The Holy Bible teaches that the ancient nation of Israel was established from the descendants of Jacob (Israel). They were initially a theocracy, governed by direct proclamations from God through Moses and Aaron and a line of priests descending from Aaron. Their living conditions vacillated between prosperity and oppression, based mainly on general adherence to the laws given by God through the priests and prophets.

When circumstances became especially difficult a leader, called a judge, arose from the people and helped them ward off the enemy of the day. Although the judges were usually not priests, they were always empowered by God for their duties.

The people survived by this method from generation to generation without a strong sense of continuity other than by their families and faith in God. They eventually tired of the lack of predictability and desired a king. Like us, they wanted to know who was in charge and who was likely to follow in each leader's wake.

This desire was said to offend God, since it represented an apparent doubt by His people that He was fully in charge or particularly concerned about them. Even so, He allowed them the freedom to choose their form of government. He also started them out on the right foot, picking an outstanding young man named Saul to be the first king of Israel.

Saul had initial success that included a string of impressive military victories. However, it is of paramount importance to note that even though the Bible says Saul was chosen by God to lead the people and was operating by His Spirit, the prior system of priests and prophets was not abolished. There was a distinct separation of the functions of religion and government in ancient Israel, with functions such as war leadership and law enforcement generally handled by the king (the civil government) and spiritual guidance and worship in the hands of the priests.

Those familiar with the Bible scriptures describing Saul's reign may recall at this point how he lost his right to govern. The Bible says that he lost it by usurping the function of the priesthood, by offering sacrifices and seeking spiritual guidance through those other than the designated priests.

After Saul's right to govern and pass government to his descendants was terminated, it was said to be passed by God's direction to David. David is described in the Bible as a prophet and one of God's favorite people. But even he was not allowed to excessively intertwine the functions of civil government and religion.

The Israelites had an elaborate box called the Ark of the Covenant that served as a symbol of God's presence among them. After Jerusalem was established as the ancient nation's capital, David determined to move the Ark into the city. God gave strict rules of transport for the Ark many years before, through Moses. The instructions were for certain priests to carry it in a certain way. David's efforts to move the Ark in a different manner resulted in violent death to one of the non-priest movers who reached up to steady it as it jostled on the moving cart. The priests moved it the rest of the way in the prescribed manner without further incident.

The remainder of the Biblical history of the Israelite kings has other similar examples. In one instance, a trip by the king into the place of priestly function resulted in his contracting the disease of leprosy.

While life was always better for the people when the king and the key government figures were righteous, the leaders did not hold the combined offices of king and priest. Thus, separation between civil and religious government functions was mandatory in ancient Israel, without benefit of a First Amendment.

The closest the separate functions came to unity was when the high priest ruled during the early reign of Josiah, who took the office of king at the age of only six. And even then, the civil and religious functions were separated, with young Josiah being directed by the high priest to make the decisions pertaining to his office.

The concept of separation was similarly established in the New Testament, even in the face of a much harsher secular government than ours has ever been, that of the Roman Empire. The words of Jesus Christ, "Render therefore unto Caesar the things which be Caesar's, and unto God the things which be God's," are a strong endorsement of the concept. The Apostle Paul also wrote part of his

Epistle to the Romans to encourage respect for the secular government and to defend its responsibility for dispensing justice.

It thus appears that the concept of separation of civil government and religion was initiated by the voice of the Eternal eons ago. Our First Amendment separation of church and state simply reflects a similarly wise policy.

Church and state separation has greatly benefited our society, and our world through that society. It should be assiduously maintained. Generally religious, predominantly Christian, people founded our nation. They were wise enough, and observant enough, to realize that a great nation of many peoples could not long survive unless the law of the land established that the government would not be allowed to institutionalize the rules of particular religious factions.

Where Religion and Government are Joined

We can see the terrible results of rejecting the wisdom of separating government and religion in countries throughout the world where religious zealots are allowed to impose their beliefs upon the populace. These countries are invariably backwards; they oppress women, minorities, and free thought.

Consider a less extreme example, the British monarchy, where the monarch is the figurehead leader of the "majesty's" government and the Church of England. Would we choose to have the royal family, from whatever era, as our moral examples?

Unfortunately, we do not have to look across the oceans to see the negative effects of merging religious and government functions. Our own criminal justice system often tends toward the nominally Christian virtues of mercy, forgiveness, rehabilitation and reconciliation.

When it becomes overly dominated by these motivations, it also becomes more of a comfort to the criminal and his or her loved ones than to the victim or our corporate society. Under such circumstances, the victim of crime is apparently supposed to forgive, especially if the criminal can be coached to mouth a brief expression of remorse, or repentance, before being sent away to mercifully serve a fraction of the sentence. We should get such religious training on our own time and not look to receive it from government.

Conflicts in Culture

Aside from the government/religious separation issue, we need to acknowledge the obvious fact that ancient Israel stands alone in history on a pedestal not shared with the United States of America. The emotional temptation through the years has been for some religious leaders, government officials and candidates for office to allege a special union between the Almighty and our government or people, considering this country to be a kind of New Jerusalem. High profile speakers have also occasionally asserted that American culture is superior to those of other nations because of Christianity's dominance in our history.

Reading <u>War and Peace</u>, the masterpiece of the Russian author, Tolstoy, shows that Americans have not been alone in such misguided pride. Misrepresentation along this line has been periodically used in attempts to whip the citizenry into frenzies of self-righteousness for or against particular political issues. A partial list of such issues (with the frenzy-whipping sometimes on both sides of the same issue) includes our American revolution, alcohol prohibition, gambling, abortion, civil rights, homosexuality and public education. Attempts have been made in all of these cases to impose some group's specific interpretation of morality, religion or Bible law upon the rest of the populace, usually with total disregard for the differing contexts between biblical times and the current American circumstances.

Before yielding our agreement to assertions about special national relationships with the Almighty and cultural superiority, we should remember that our culture has benefited greatly from others of different backgrounds. We have African, Arabic and Asian cultures to thank for the inventions of such basics of our existence as usable numbers, paper and gunpowder. It is democracy, and the participation of the religious and non-religious within it, which has freed our souls to worship in physical peace, our minds to think and invent, our capital to produce and the women and minority groups of our nation to contribute. All of these factors have combined to cause our society to excel. You do not have to be a math genius to understand that a society that denies meaningful participation to its women and minorities condemns itself to operating with less than half of its potential creative power.

While Christianity may save the soul, it does not save the government. Christianity was the official religion of the Roman Empire when it fell. America was not founded as and has not developed into a Christian nation. This fact has contributed to our existence as the earth's oldest and most prosperous democracy. This is not to say that an American's inner religious scruples should be excluded from his or her outer decision-making. Those scruples and motivations certainly should come into play on the basis of individual conscience, with each person free to voluntarily associate with others of like mind for corporate expression, whether religious or political. For example, slavery was morally wrong as well as socially wrong and economically inefficient, and those who joined together, by whatever motivation, to rid our nation of that curse served us well.

However, no group has legitimate moral authority to coerce fellow citizens into an involuntary association or recognition of religion or thought. No group can legitimately demand that the United States of America, as God's country, must reach any particular political conclusion. For our thanks should ever ring as high as heaven that the authorizing document of law in this nation is not the Bible, or the Koran or the Book of Mormon. Individuals are free to govern their personal lives by those or other standards of religious belief and behavior within the context of this land's foundational document, our Constitution.

Bible Law

Those who seek to have Bible law established usually do not understand what they say they want. Ancient Israel's method of capital punishment was typically stoning, and it was readily imposed. Examples of capital crimes noted in the Bible include picking up sticks on the Sabbath day and rebelling against parents. Activities described as "abominable" to God included the eating of pork and numerous other foods that many Americans enjoy. Who can say with a straight face that they would like such laws enforced in America? Certainly there is no such person of any credibility. People may presume that God had His reasons for establishing such laws in ancient Israel. However, we can also be thankful that they are not our corporate burdens to bear.

Even so, it would seem that a devout Christian making the error of attempting to apply biblical mandates to society, rather than his or her own personal life, would choose the commandments of Jesus Christ. He told us to judge not, that we be not judged, establishing the illegitimacy of claims of moral superiority of one over another. He also specifically said to turn the other cheek, to not even resist evil acts against us: not even physical attacks or unjust lawsuits that would take the clothes off our backs. He also commanded that we ignore our impulses for the comforts of this life. He held the selfishness of some wealthy people up as examples worthy of scorn as he commanded us to pour out our fortunes and our lives for the benefit of the needy. His willingness to accept torturous death at the hands of the entrenched powers of His day proves just how seriously He took His own words.

Even so, adoption of the true commands of Jesus Christ by society as a whole under the law of man would be as ridiculous as the attempted imposition of the previously mentioned stonings. In domestic policy, it could create a nation of sheep among wolves, with no legal redress for acts of cruelty and no right of self-defense. Foreign policy would be the same. How could such a nation even defend itself, much less the freedoms of the rest of the world, as we did in World Wars I and II and throughout the Cold War, and are now doing again by mobilizing against international terrorist organizations?

As an individual, one may feel religiously compelled to turn the other cheek. But civil government operating in proper balance, disentangled from religion, should impose no such duty. Mutual protection is the main reason that our ancestors came forth from the individuality of their caves and forests to form societies. In a balanced society, we could decline to individually resist evil in confidence that we would all vigorously resist it together through the structure of our united civil authority.

The crux of the matter is this: it is not in the interest of people or God to seek union of human civil and religious authority. Neither the United States Constitution nor the Holy Bible sanctions, or even encourages, such a union. We would do well to heed the advice from the mouth of Jesus Christ about rendering appropriately to Caesar and to God.

And the fortunate corollary to that instruction for the American citizen is that, in this nation, Caesar is not he or they. We are "Caesar." It is our government and it is our sovereign right apart from that government to choose our God or gods and manners of worship according to conscience, with the combined government of our citizenry entitled to overrule religious practices only in the most extreme circumstances.

We will undoubtedly continue to debate from time to time whether the current specific level of separation is too great or small. Nevertheless, so long as we recognize the validity of the basic principle of religious and government separation under our Constitution, no pendulum swing of political change during any generation will take us very far from the balance that we need.

Some specific issues are particularly controversial as of the time of this writing, with their bases in the sincere religious beliefs of millions of citizens. The most divisive include abortion, homosexual rights, and the public schools, especially with regard to the Pledge of Allegiance and prayer.

2. Abortion

The emotional fuel of the persistently vocal, and sometimes violent, anti-abortion rights movement is a sincerely held moral belief that an abortion is taught by God through the Bible to be a murder. However, if a good faith biblical interpretation can lead to a conclusion that it may not be murder, it would seem that the associated emotionalism might be overstated.

What the Bible Says

From the way that many anti-abortion rights protesters conduct themselves, a person not familiar with the Holy Bible would think it loaded with passages equating abortion with murder. However, this is not the case. The passages that are most frequently cited are open to significant interpretive leeway.

The writer of Psalm 139 refers to himself as being "fearfully and wonderfully made" by God, with each detail known before the time of birth. An interesting aspect of this passage as recorded in the King James Version of the Bible is that it refers to the place of the psalm writer's having been made as "the depths of the earth" as well as the womb. The obvious question here is whether the writer is referring to a time prior to the conception of human life in the womb, possibly all the way back to the biblical description of the formation of the first man, Adam, from the earth.

If the passage should be taken as relating back to Adam, it would reflect a mandate for emphasizing the dignity of all human life, rather than one focusing on pre-born life in the womb. The Catholic Church has accepted this total human dignity approach. While its official position has been against almost all abortion rights, it has also been in favor of laws requiring higher wages for workers and more adequate social support for the weak. If the entire anti-abortion rights movement were as consistent, it might have more credibility with the general public.

A second key passage is in the Gospel of Luke. It refers to John the Baptist, a cousin of Jesus Christ. This was the prophet that the New Testament says was sent to announce Christ's coming. The unborn John is described as "leaping" for joy in the womb of his mother, Elizabeth (about six months pregnant at the time), when Mary, the expectant mother of Jesus, came into their presence.

A third set of frequently cited passages includes the references to Mary being "with child," as the pregnancy was described. The messages from anti-abortion rights groups are that such passages, plus the biological fact that, from the moment of conception, there is a dividing mass of living cells containing all the chromosomal information needed to result in a mature human (and which increasingly resembles a mature human as gestation progresses), undoubtedly establish that abortion is murder. Many holding this opinion consequently believe that use of any available means is warranted to rescue the pre-born life.

There are some very real problems with practical implementation of this opinion. But before discussing them, some other interesting passages, also from the Bible, should be considered.

The first is in chapter 21 of the Hebrew Bible book of Exodus. The passage is in a section where Moses was said to be receiving judgments on various issues of civil law straight from God, in the time period previously described as ancient Israel before the kings. Recall that at that time God directly governed the people through the priests.

The passage indicates that if men were fighting and one of their wives intervened and, being pregnant, was injured by her husband's adversary to the extent that she miscarried, the injurer was to compensate the father with money. It appears that in this ancient farming society the father was to be compensated for loss of a potential familial farmhand or housekeeper.

However, the case was clearly not considered murder, for the penalty for murder was death. Nor was it considered manslaughter, or negligent killing of a human, for the penalty established for that crime was banishment to a specified location until the death of the high priest living at the time of the offense.

Another Hebrew Bible passage, Numbers chapter 5, is also interesting. In this case, a husband who suspected his wife of adultery was instructed to bring her to the priest, who made her drink a special concoction. If she was guilty of infidelity, the King James Version of the Bible says that the mixture would cause her "thigh to rot and her belly to swell." Such a physical condition would undoubtedly result in a miscarriage for a pregnant woman. This can either be taken to indicate that a mystical result of the procedure came to pass, or that any pregnancy would have been terminated by it. But in either case, a legitimate question arises as to whether the priest was instructed to preside over the abortion of an illegitimate child. One can reach a good faith interpretation that indeed he was.

It may also be of consequence that the angels sang before the shepherds upon Jesus' birth, rather than upon His conception. Along that same line, I have yet to meet the person who dates the beginning of his or her life at nine months before emergence from the womb. A teenager anxiously awaiting a driver's license would be unwise to try that argument. At any rate, it is easy to see that a good faith interpretation of the Bible does not have to equate abortion with murder, or even manslaughter.

However, even if one takes the interpretation that the Bible forbids abortion as murder, it can also be seen as forbidding other things in much more definite terms; such as divorce, Sabbath work, missing church and overeating. Although short-lived attempts are periodically made to impose limits against such activities on our entire society, they have invariably been abandoned because (1) enforcement of such laws is next to impossible, and (2) the vast majority of us believe such things are nobody's business but our own. Thus, it is in the area of practical application that the anti-abortion rights argument collapses.

Practical Problems

The basic premise of the anti-abortion rights position is that a human life, absolutely as valuable and relevant as that of any person ever born, results at the instant that the male sperm and female egg unite in conception. We can no longer add the phrase "in the body of the mother," as has been seen in legal battles involving frozen embryos created under laboratory conditions. Such cases consume much public money and time before the obvious conclusion is inevitably reached that the embryos are not people.

The unreasonable nature of an absolutist opinion is not only exposed by incidents made possible by modern technology. In a small percentage of pregnancies, the fertilized egg will implant in a place other than in the womb, such as in a uterine tube or an ovary. This is known as an ectopic pregnancy. The condition is generally fatal, not only concerning the life of the developing embryo but, also, for the female in which it is developing if she is not treated by termination of the pregnancy. Almost everyone, including those supposedly holding absolutist anti-abortion views, would agree in such a case that the pregnancy should be immediately terminated to save the woman's life. However, such a termination is inconsistent with the viewpoint that the biblical commandment of "thou shalt not kill" applies from the moment of conception. How can one justify termination of any innocent life, even to save another?

Who Is Being Defended Against?

An argument of self-defense is usually posed to justify abortions for ectopic pregnancies, as it is in other cases in which the life of a female is endangered by pregnancy. However, a look beneath the surface of this position reveals it to be a rationalization based on political factors rather than credible principals of morality or law.

The right to self-defense is based on a legal doctrine reserved for situations where an individual who is acting (or is reasonably thought to be acting) to do personal bodily harm to another is hurt or killed by the victim or another person defending on behalf of the victim. Additionally, the threatened person must not have provoked or precipitated the threat.

No such attempt to harm is being made by the ectopic embryo or, for that matter, by an embryo that happens to be developing in the womb and causing untoward medical complications in the pregnant female. Nor can the pregnant female or her "defending" physician reasonably believe that it is trying to harm her. It is merely existing and developing pursuant to the dictates of Divine Providence, presumably in the providentially designated place.

Furthermore, the pregnant female must be considered to have taken part in precipitating the threat if the pregnancy resulted from consensual sex between adults. Voluntary precipitation of the threat generally undermines a legitimate claim to a fully excused right to lethal self-defense.

Persons who would persist in claiming that a right to self-defense exists in such cases despite the voluntary precipitation of the threat should at least acknowledge that the Almighty, not the developing embryo, is the only one against whom exercise of such a right may reasonably be directed. To contend otherwise would be the same as arguing that the right of self-defense against an armed attacker should be exercised against the bullet in the chamber rather than against the person with a finger on the trigger. The only position that is morally and legally consistent with an absolutist anti-abortion philosophy is to let the woman die a harsh death, almost simultaneously with the ectopic embryo.

The response will surely come that such a position is unreasonable since the unborn life will perish anyway. However, to expose the flawed logic of the absolutist opinion, we must carry it to its illogical conclusions.

Thus, the common law doctrine of self-defense must be stretched beyond credible recognition to use it to rationalize termination of a pregnancy threatening a woman's health. But there is a common law doctrine that is readily applicable to such a situation if one is serious about equalizing rights and responsibilities between the born and the unborn. It relates to the duty of a parent to protect his or her child.

A Relevant Legal Doctrine

There is no common law duty to rescue a stranger in trouble, such as a drowning child. However, there is a common law duty to make reasonable attempts to rescue, based upon relationship, in the case of parent and child. The "parent," the pregnant female, thus would have a duty to try to rescue her unborn "child" if this premise were applied.

In keeping with the absolutist position, strangers have waged well-publicized legal battles to prevent families from disconnecting hopelessly comatose relatives from mechanical life support systems. They reason that each second of "life," no matter how devoid of function or experience, is immeasurably precious. Consider another type of case that gains publicity from time to time, in which a pregnant woman is injured and loses decision-making capacity. A husband that consults with physicians and decides to seek an abortion in order to give his wife her best chance at survival may find himself facing unfamiliar parties holding an absolutist opinion in court, seeking guardianship of the comatose wife (alleging that she is incompetent to agree to an abortion) and the fetus (alleging that its right to life is about to be violated). The husband and the rest of her family would thus be dragged through the legal system, under very difficult circumstances and with time very much at issue, before being allowed to terminate the pregnancy.

Let us accept that it is not reasonable to require that a woman give her life for another, even her child. Even so, should those holding an absolutist position not seek to require the pregnant mother to do her "duty" to rescue her unborn child, to allow it to live to the last incalculably precious second, up until the imminent approach of her own death? Should this not especially be the case in light of the likelihood that, at least in America, her condition will be closely monitored in a modern hospital, where advanced technology can allow the unborn child to wring the last drop of gusto from its short, but dramatic, life? And should the absolutist interpretation not consider the associated suffering of the woman of little consequence in light of the continuation of the life of the ectopic or otherwise health-threatening embryo in her body? The morally consistent answer to each of these questions would seem to be yes.

A Clash of Two Lives

The most telling indictment against the absolutist philosophy comes in the cases where the question is whether to abort to preserve the life of the mother. Almost all parties holding absolutist opinions adhere to the exception of allowing abortion in such cases. Allowing an abortion to save the life of the mother is simply a value judgment that the life of the born is of more worth than that of the unborn.

This is exactly the same value judgment for which those favoring preservation of abortion rights are sometimes criticized. The question is merely a matter of degree rather than a competition between holy light and devilish darkness, as some prefer to cast it. In reality, it is a competition between competing shades of grey, with one faction more willing to attribute to government the wisdom to make decisions concerning child bearing than to the person bearing the child.

Political expediency requires the absolutist position to agree to allow exceptions to the desired ban on all abortions in cases of rape or incest in addition to threats to the life of the mother. Even if one rejects the previous examples concerning ectopic or frozen embryos and comatose mothers as unrealistic or too infrequent to matter, it is certain that a developing embryo, a human "life," had no voice in how it was conceived. As the Holy Scriptures say, the children should not suffer for the sins of the fathers.

So, the existence of the rape and incest exceptions within the absolutist framework is inconsistent. The basis for the exceptions is pure political compromise, a necessity in order to keep the number of adherents for the anti-abortion rights position from shrinking to near zero.

A Question of Privacy

So, what is a balanced position on abortion rights? The initial wisdom of the often-attacked <u>Roe v. Wade</u> decision of the Supreme Court is difficult to improve upon. It set forth the principle that government interest in the abortion decision ranged from low to high over time based upon the stage of gestation and viability of the fetus. The scope of the original decision has been modified by subsequent decisions over time. Yet, the foundational presumption that it established remains, that the responsibility for an abortion decision is primarily left with the pregnant female and her doctor, where it belongs.

We should also remember the legal basis from which the <u>Roe</u> decision developed. It was based on a constitutional "right to privacy" which began to be officially established by the Supreme Court in the 1960s by way of a case called <u>Griswold v. Connecticut</u>. It may be hard for many to believe now, but the <u>Griswold</u> decision resulted from a state law that made it illegal for citizens, including married adults, to use contraception.

To this day, when someone attacks legal construction upholding a constitutional right to privacy, the person is indicating that he or she believes that the state or federal government should be able to order the citizenry to not use contraception, or not engage in any other private activity, even those activities consensually performed in the marital bed. Thus, they place government rights to police private intimate behavior at least on a par with other rights and above most, even those associated with the institution of marriage, which predated our Constitution and government by thousands of years. And it should be obvious to anyone willing to think that if a person agrees with government encroachment upon the marital bed, or the maternal body, that any other type of invasion of privacy would be considered of no consequence at all. Every passing year's advances in technology should make all of us shudder the more at the thought of an unfettered governmental capacity to monitor, and judge, our private business.

Such a cavalier attitude about personal privacy is also a fairly good indication that the person attacking the right to privacy has not read the Constitution, or may have read it with such blinders on that only the parts agreed with registered. For it is clearly stated in the Ninth Amendment that, "The enumeration in the Constitution, of certain rights, shall not be construed to deny or disparage others retained by the people." Thus, the founders had no intention of pretending to set forth the definitive list of the rights of all Americans for all generations.

Their recognition of their own shortcomings would not allow them to engage in such arrogance. They also had a hearty number of detractors to remind them of their fallibility if they dared to slip into forgetfulness. And the historical fact is that one of the arguments against addition of a Bill of Rights to the Constitution was the very fear that misguided individuals would construe the listed rights as all-inclusive. Modern day opponents of an interpretation of the U.S. Constitution that includes privacy rights show a lack of flexibility and empathy that the opponents to the Bill of Rights feared might materialize.

The arrogance of the anti-privacy position is consistent with the opinions of some who feel qualified to act as self-appointed guardians of "life" as they interfere with painful family decisions concerning comatose family members and pre-born potential family members. And, of course, this interference can sometimes come from a comfortable distance, only requiring occasional appearances before the courts and the press. Unfortunately, those who personally agonize over these decisions do not have the option of escape. They must continue to cope with the day-to-day responsibilities of decisions involving their family members long after interlopers have moved on.

Perhaps the greatest irony of this situation is that some who would do away with a constitutional right to privacy double as leaders in the charge to "get government off our backs." The debate surrounding and recent passage of the late term ("partial-birth") abortion ban is a perfect example of questionable motivations from both ends of the political spectrum. Knee-jerk abortion and privacy rights supporters marginalized their standing with the great majority of the public when they would not accept a widely popular restriction that, if properly drafted, would have fit comfortably within the <u>Roe v. Wade</u> framework. On the other hand, some knee-jerk abortion and privacy rights opponents were so intransigent as to refuse to include a "health of the mother" exception to an otherwise reasonable restriction, thus dooming the law to probably be overturned in the courts.

Child-bearing and Child-rearing

Under the same reasoning by which we should continue to limit government access to private decisions on child bearing, we should similarly deny government access into family matters relative to child rearing. The resistance by some abortion rights supporters against laws preventing performance of an abortion for a minor dependent child without notification to and permission from the girl's parents is based upon a presumption that the state has more care and concern for her than her parents.

The premise that the impersonal mechanism of the state is capable of showing more concern for a child than her parents is absurd on its face. Government at its best is almost always inferior to parents at their worst. Besides what should be a nearly overwhelming presumption that the parents, not the government, care most for the girl, the parents have the additional interest created by their having maintained the living expenses of a dependent minor daughter.

The anti-parental notification position represents another misguided attempt to mingle the religious virtues of mercy and compassion with the administrative and judicial functions of government. The state is ill equipped to operate upon the broad field of emotion.

Government's role in abortion decisions for dependent minors should, therefore, be very narrowly limited to situations of absolute necessity, such as where there is dependable documentation of a history of abuse of the child. A dependent child's non-parent advocate should be able to petition a court to obtain necessary permission for the procedure without parental notification only in such extreme cases. Parental notification requirements should not restrict a minor emancipated from dependence on her parents if she can establish her independence before a court.

The voices of non-custodial parents should also be considered, but with a degree of weight which corresponds to the degree of care previously shown by that parent. A non-custodial parent who has failed to previously engage in adequate exercise of parental responsibilities should not be able to exercise a veto over an abortion decision reached by the custodial parent and their daughter. The process of weighing a contested right of non-custodial parental input is also an issue for the courts.

By the same token, the "morning after pill," which undoubtedly induces a very early term abortion, should not be available over-the-counter. Government's interest at such an early point after conception is minimal. However, parents have a right, and responsibility, to be involved in their minor daughters' use of such medications, and keeping it out of over-the-counter distribution is a reasonable governmental recognition and support of that right.

The topic of abortion generates a higher level of emotion than almost any other issue. Emotion has a tendency to decrease the ability to reasonably consider and solve problems.

Even if one believes abortion to be murder, it must be conceded that American political support does not exist to legislate a morally consistent (total) abortion ban. Nor is such support likely to develop in the future, despite the use of rationalizations to attempt to justify political compromise for cases of rape, incest and danger to the mother's life.

Citizens morally opposed to abortion would serve society well by seeking to prevent, rather than preserve, unwanted conceptions. This can be done by encouragement of strong parent-child relationships, education and availability of birth control.

The right to privacy is a valid one that should not be lightly violated. Similarly, the right to full parental involvement in cases of pregnant, minor, dependent daughters should be avidly protected.

Our society needs to accept a balanced position on this issue and others related to dignity of life that acknowledges the primacy of personal conscience and medically guided family judgment in private matters. The sooner we do, the sooner we can turn the considerable energy expended in arguing about them to more productive directions.

3. Homosexuality

A second very divisive issue of current religious/political involvement is homosexuality. Millions refer to the story about the towns of Sodom and Gomorrah, which the Bible tells us were destroyed by God with fire (at least in part because many of their inhabitants were involved in same-sex behavior), as a warning against a society's allowing such behavior. As with abortion, the passions run so deep on this issue that reason and balance are often shouted down. Nevertheless, if we calm down enough to stop and think, we can find balance.

What Remedy?

For those who hold the opinion that same-sex behavior is "abominable" to God (the same description given in the King James Version of the Bible book of Isaiah for His view of the eating of pork) and must be eradicated to keep the nation from the same fate as Sodom and Gomorrah, the question of remedy is begged. The Bible teaches in the Old Testament that the punishment for same-sex behavior was execution (as it was on at least one occasion for picking up sticks on the Sabbath day, among many other offenses). Maybe a few misguided people believe that such a reaction is appropriate for today's America. Fortunately, only a very few believe this, and even fewer would admit having such an attitude.

The record of the life of Jesus Christ in the New Testament does not reveal a preoccupation with same-sex behavior. His focus was much more upon what people did with their money than with what they did in private personal relations. Although the writings of the Apostle Paul can be interpreted as listing same-sex behavior as potential grounds for eternal condemnation (among numerous others), he did not suggest that it, or a propensity for it, should be used as a basis to deny a job. As is always the case, judgment of personal religious matters should be reserved to God, individual conscience and church bodies with respect to their membership, not government.

To the extent that governments might claim a public welfare interest relative to the AIDS disease crisis in monitoring or preventing private consensual homosexual activity between adults, consistency should require that they also assert a public welfare interest in monitoring consensual heterosexual activity between adults relative to other sexually transmitted diseases and the break-up of homes due to adultery. However, the far better path, and the only practically enforceable one, is for the government to leave the people alone in the area of consensual adult sexuality.

Expression or Existence?

Some medical studies have suggested that there is an inborn genetic propensity for homosexuality, that is, to have a sexual desire for the same sex rather than the opposite. If it is a matter of genetics, it is a matter of existence.

Issues of existence are separate from those of expression, or the acting out of one's existence. One must exist to express, but one need not express to exist.

The Supreme Court ruled in 1986 in the Bowers v. Hardwick case that states could enforce laws making homosexual acts between consenting adults illegal.

That decision was recently overturned in another case, <u>Texas v. Lawrence</u>. These decisions were based primarily on a privacy rights analysis, but the <u>Lawrence</u> case did begin to frame the issue in terms of expression.

Forms of symbolic or verbal expression relating to one's homosexuality are entitled to no more or less protection under First Amendment freedom of speech than any other form of similar expression. Thus, even considering such expression under the high level of protection afforded under the First Amendment, a private employer is not limited under the Constitution from terminating the employment of a person publicly expressing homosexuality because the act of the private employer does not constitute a state action which is subject to the prohibitions of the Constitution.

Our Constitution certainly protects the right to express, within the confines of reasonable time, place and manner restrictions. Such restrictions make it just as inappropriate for a public school teacher to voice or exhibit homosexually oriented expression while on the job as it would be to voice or exhibit heterosexually oriented expression on the job, even though any discipline engaged in by the public school administration in the matter would be state action. Thus, it can reasonably be required that such expression be restrained as a condition of employment.

Similarly, the courts have left little doubt that homosexual expression by military personnel, whether by words or acts, can be legitimately suppressed by the state action of military decision-making, at least during duty hours. This is particularly the case since the Supreme Court has already decided that military personnel have no constitutional right to engage in overt religious expression during duty.

Nor can the United States Constitution be used in a manner with a credible historical basis to require states to take an active supporting role in the furtherance of homosexual expression, such as by requiring the granting of marriage licenses. An individual can no more reasonably expect an active state endorsement of his or her expression of sexuality than could an artist legitimately expect to use the Constitution to require the government to fund his artistic expression.

Nor does the Constitution create a historically supportable foundation for providing a captive audience for homosexual expression by way of requiring equal rights to adopt children. This is particularly the case with the best interests of the child being the main criteria for adoption. There is ample objective data to prove, and no way to disprove, that the best interests of children are most strongly met in a stable male-female parental setting.

The people are free to decide through the legislative branches of the state and federal governments that the homosexual expression described in each of these examples should be legally protected. State courts can also interpret State Constitutions to provide such rights for citizens of individual states. But the United States Constitution does not require it. And, as the law now stands, individual states are no more required to respect homosexual marriages granted in another state than they are common law marriages granted in another state. These matters are properly left to the individual states. Thus, there does not appear to be a need to amend our U.S. Constitution to define marriage.

Marriage is regulable by the several states for perfectly legitimate reasons. Unlike homosexual unions, marriage creates a forum between a couple, in and of their relationship, whereby children may be born. The state is thereby justified in using marriage to create obligations and rights for support, if for no other reason than protecting the public treasury. Such common sense rationales are why state prohibitions against marriage between very close relatives are legally sound, why national preclusion of polygamy has stood the test of time, and why preclusion of extension of federal marriage rights to same-sex couples through the Defense of Marriage Act is likely to withstand legal challenge. The Supreme Court's Texas v. Lawrence decision that reversed Bowers v. Hardwick was a wise endorsement of the right to privacy.

Contrary to the concern arising over Texas v. Lawrence from some quarters, there is no reason for this case to lead to gay marriage. It does not mandate marriage rights, which should rightly remain under the auspices of the states and the churches. Rather, it just endorses the rights of consenting adults to be left alone by the government with regard to their non-assaultive private sexual behaviors.

On the other hand, the Texas v. Lawrence decision does not require nor make the case for recognition of homosexual "civil unions," as some have argued. The justifications for civil unions are usually cast in emotionally charged terms relating to inheritance, hospital visitations for comatose people and health insurance coverage. However, will, living will and power of attorney laws can already accommodate inheritance, hospital visitations and the handling of affairs during incapacitation. Where the law does not satisfy relevant concerns, the legislative process is available to remedy the situation according to the usual standards.

But, I do have a more personal point of opposition on the health insurance issue. When I was in my 20s, I was the primary breadwinner for a household including my mother and several younger siblings. I would have liked to have those family members who were financially dependent on me covered under my employer-paid health insurance but was not allowed to do so under the policy.

Should those entering into a voluntary non-marriage relationship, a "civil union," be accorded more protections under the law with regard to insurance than dependent blood family members, including dependent children? I think not.

Perhaps broadening the head of household classification for federal income taxation purposes would make sense to allow some relief for persons supporting dependents in their own households, whether biologically or adoptively related or not. But the civil union concept has the potential to unnecessarily cloud up all kinds of interactions, from insurance coverage to inheritance, with regard to blood relations who by traditional notions of societal responsibility and common decency have some reasonable expectation of support. Therefore, legal recognition of civil unions is a bad idea, without regard to sexual orientation, although states do have the right to decide otherwise through their legislative processes. I just personally consider the concept a political contrivance without credible merit.

Where Government Should Fear to Tread

Even if the premise is accepted that homosexuality is a matter of existence, rather than a tendency that may lead to expression (a premise that has not nearly gained unanimous scientific consent), we should consider analogous matters of existence to determine the proper interrelation of the government and the citizenry on the subject. Some assert that homosexuality is on a par with other existence issues, such as gender, race and age, and that it should consequently be accorded equal Constitutional protection under the law.

However, homosexuality is actually more similar to religion than to these other existence issues because neither homosexuality nor religion can be readily discerned by others without identifying expression. Homosexuality is also patently different from religion in that one of the founding motivations for the settlement of the North American continent was to escape religious persecution then existing in Europe. Consequently, religion has been appropriately accorded specific First Amendment protection under the Constitution. Only the most optimistic of homosexual rights advocates expect that homosexuality will ever achieve similar status by way of constitutional amendment.

The confusion that has been generated by many Supreme Court rulings on religion shows that government is ill-equipped to establish new legal protections or prohibitions based on existence factors which cannot be readily discerned without inquiring into defining expressions. Our society does not substantially suffer from the incessant arguments over who can pray where and when and over what religious symbols can be displayed at what time and place and in what manner, because of the universal acknowledgement of the importance of the subject matter.

However, leaders are extremely ill advised when they suggest that we need to engage in such societal line drawing relative to another area of difficult to discern existence issues. This will continue to be so even if future scientific evidence agrees upon the legitimacy of the existence argument unless means can also be developed to easily discern homosexual status on an objective basis.

Some citizens are more than willing to police the private consensual sexual behaviors of their adult neighbors. We can be sure that those same individuals would take offense if someone tried to do it to them. However, most of us can agree that government best serves the people in matters of consensual adult sexuality when it observes the passive responsibility of respecting the privacy of the citizenry and declines to take on active responsibilities that it cannot effectively carry out. We can hope and work toward assuring that future decisions of the judicial, legislative and executive branches of government will reflect such common sense.

4. The Pledge of Allegiance

Like the national motto, which was changed from "E Pluribus Unum" to "In God We Trust," the Pledge got a religious upgrade in the middle of the last century with the addition of the phrase "under God."

Whether or not changing the Pledge was sincere or wise is of no consequence at this point. The Pledge says what it says, and it has said it the same for some 50 years. It is not a prayer or religious inculcation. It has a secular citizenship purpose and nobody has to say it. Its religious significance is entirely in the eyes and hearts of the beholders, perhaps akin to the slight possibility that someone might consider American dollars holy because "In God We Trust" is inscribed upon them. We all know that the dollar that circulates its way into the church collection plate next Sunday may well have secured the services of the prostitute or drug dealer the week before. Consequently, it was no surprise when the Supreme Court correctly decided in 2004 to let the current wording for the Pledge stand, albeit in a passive way that potentially left the issue open for future litigation.

5. The Public Schools

The ambivalence of some about the wording of the Pledge of Allegiance gives a perfect lead into some discussion on the public schools. The public schools are critical to the continued success of this nation, and many of them are failing, caught in the equivalent of a military pincer maneuver between selfish people, some of whom seem unwilling to pay for necessaries and others who do not seem to be willing to acknowledge a need for discipline and order in a learning environment. The two factions actually play off one another, with the first refusing to pay until the environment is improved and the second using lack of money as an excuse to refuse to pressure for improvement in the environment. And the kids and their parents are caught in the middle.

There are few more important responsibilities for government than restoring these schools to strength so that children can learn what they need to know in a physically, emotionally and spiritually secure environment. I include spiritually in the list because parents have just as much right to expect that their minor children are not having their religions undermined by the government as they do to expect that the children are not being religiously indoctrinated. The public schools need to stick to fundamentals of well-rounded knowledge, skills and citizenship, and leave the questioning of foundations to college and university settings after students become young adults and are able to begin to execute mature thought.

The U.S. Department of Education has provided some very good guidelines to show the wide range of student religious activities that are proper in the public school context. However, these guidelines do not prevent religion-based lawsuits. The schools typically do not have the spare money to fend them off, so they are pressured to take the path of least resistance and overcompensate against religious expression. This is an unacceptable outcome.

Considering the overriding secular imperative that the government has in maintaining a strong public school system, federal funding of public school legal defense could be appropriate, whether the lawsuits stem from religion or other causes. This would reduce financial pressure on the schools. Being able to hire experienced First Amendment litigators would also improve chances for the schools to prevail in court, resulting in a more balanced pattern of school administrator behavior.

The public schools need those children and parents back in the system that have left it for sectarian academies and home schooling. Most of those parents could better use the time and the money that they are now double-spending on education (counting their taxes and school tuitions). But, they will not come back until they are confident that there are no threats of anti-religious undermining or to reasonable physical safety.

Prayer in the schools is often the main focus of the public school dispute. It was not unusual for classes to pray in the public schools I attended more than three decades ago. It did not seem to be a particularly significant event in the day, but we did usually all become quiet at the same time, so it may have been more significant than it appeared through the eyes of a child.

What of Minority Christian Children?

It seems at first blush to be an overreaction on the part of the anti-religious or holders of minority religions to be allowed to deny the majority an exercise that has significant symbolic value, and that may do some good. However, when thinking about this issue, I cannot help but recall some children in my classes during the early years of school.

They were smart, well dressed and well behaved. However, they were from a family that adhered to a very strict Christian religious sect that frowned on dancing. When the rest of the students were directed to perform some children's dance, they always declined.

As an adult I can look back and admire the courage of those children for adhering to the religious principles taught at home. However, as children, most of us did not understand that they were admirable. They were merely different. And in being so bold as to be different, they became targets for the types of meanness in which children sometimes specialize.

The school had no religious or anti-religious motive for having dances in the class. The purpose was entirely secular, similar to the citizenship basis for having the Pledge of Allegiance recited in public schools. The only reasonable option in such cases remains having religiously offended children to opt out of the secular activities. However, good conscience should preclude adult advocacy of a specifically religious social policy that would force young children to decline participation in activities concerning the deepest motivational forces that we know, such as prayer.

Parental Responsibility

There is an even stronger reason to reject the political pressure of those who advocate a return to state sponsored prayer in the public schools. The reason is that parents should not be allowed to foist their responsibilities for child rearing, such as religious and moral training, upon the government.

Some polls on the subject have indicated that more than two out of three Americans favor daily state-sponsored prayer in public schools. However, does anywhere near that percentage of parents pray with their children at home on a daily basis? Twenty percent is probably a generous estimate. Forget the daily basis. Ask the question based on a weekly basis (at home, not at church) or even a monthly basis, including meals.

The implication is that the initial reaction of some parents is that they want the public schools to be several times more religiously oriented than the private homes. However, our people are far too wise, upon steady reflection, to follow such a misguided policy. After pausing to think, we will realize that when seventy percent of parents start having daily prayer with their children, the hue and cry for prayer in the public schools will have long since passed, because the behavioral problems that led to the desires for state-sponsored prayers will also have vanished, as if by a long prayed for miracle.

We need to recognize that state sponsored prayer in the public schools is likely to be offensive to members of minority Christian denominations as well as to those holding minority non-Christian religions or no religion. Parents of public school educated children should be able to have confidence that any school activity that religiously offends them or their child will not have a religious motivation.

Parents are free to pray with their children before and after school hours, and religiously motivated children are free to meet with each other to pray during non-instructional time, much like members of other school groups are. There is no good reason to seek to amend the Constitution to guarantee rights that already exist.

And there is certainly no good reason to amend it in order to encourage religiously motivated behaviors on the part of elected officials, public school teachers and administrators. The work of religious instruction is far too important to be delegated from parents and churches to the government.

6. A Modern Shibboleth

One great American shibboleth since the late twentieth century has been the phrase, family values. The term is a true shibboleth, a code phrase with little real meaning, since it cannot be defined to general satisfaction, not even among those who wish to impose "family values," or some equally vague variation thereof, as the law of the land. My understanding of the phrase equates it with emphasizing, by law, biblical morality in today's society. Some of the practical difficulties with such efforts have already been discussed.

However, the motivations of the great majority of advocates of family values are pure. These citizens are moved by concerns over declining morality and courtesy, and increasing crime and laziness, that are threats to a country that they love as much as any other citizen, and which have become apparent in every town in America.

Values for Government Participation

The values of charity, fidelity and industry over which the broad umbrella of "family values" spreads can, and should, be encouraged by government for reasons totally disconnected from religion. These are the values of our farmland heritage, developed through the necessity of long days of hard labor and the oversight of small communities, where an atheist may work just as hard as his Christian neighbor, but where distinctions of faith can disappear in united efforts to help a person in need.

The decrease in the prevalence of these three values has roughly corresponded to the increasing urbanization and mechanization, and resulting depersonalization, of society. It may be that the encouragement of creative approaches designed to enhance the spirit of community among us, such as building homes for the poor or otherwise volunteering to help the needy, can be a helpful government contribution towards strengthening the societal foundation for developing such positive values throughout our land.

But, it certainly does not help to create a sense of community, that power of accountability and belonging from which positive social values flow, to create implied classes of religious haves and have-nots. This is the unintended result of political calls for "family values." The sooner political leaders of all factions cease trying to use this shibboleth for partisan gain, the better off we will all be.

FREEDOM FROM WANT

The first two freedoms, of speech and religion, are foundational for the first freedom from something, freedom from want. The fact that speech, communication of ideas, has been relatively unhindered in this nation has allowed the productive thoughts arising from all areas of society to enter the field of debate and result in better, more want-free, lives for all. While the past denial of the vote to black citizens and all women robbed us of their contributions for too long, those costly errors have now been renounced, changing with the inevitable tide flowing toward more speech and participation, not less. Thus, we can anticipate a future marked by growing numbers of benefits and conveniences born and perfected due to the increasingly free exchange of ideas.

Similarly, the freedom of religion releases our minds to think of ways to progress, rather than using our mental energy to dread capture or condemnation for holding personal religious beliefs. It also spares us both the loss of productive citizens by bloodshed and the enormous financial expense involved in the sustained religious wars that dominate many countries. Money spent on weapons with which to kill the "infidels" cannot be used to buy the necessities or luxuries of life.

Even though the first two freedoms are foundational, the desire for freedom from want will take precedence in the lives of many citizens over desire for the freedoms of speech and religion. Indeed, failure to establish freedom from want can result in reduction in the quality of exercise of the freedoms of speech and religion to the angry or desperate howls of the needy. Freedom from want thus creates an atmosphere in which the exercise of the freedoms of speech and religion may be elevated to the places of dignity which they deserve, and from which they can further enhance freedom from want.

1. The "Self-Made Man"

Perspective can be a wonderful thing if it is broad enough to provide an accurate picture. Consider the young man who had the expenses of his birth paid for through the shared risk system of health insurance. His parents fed and clothed him, and kept him away from fires too hot and waters too deep. He was educated in the public schools and had grades good enough to be admitted to one of our fine state universities, where he received government student loan support. Dozens of teachers and professors patiently helped him to learn his lessons and meet his requirements along the way. He and his sweetheart graduated, were married after a few years and were able to purchase a home with a small down payment thanks to a subsidized loan program. They sit down to breakfast on a typical morning over a table spread with plenty due to a stable and broadly subsidized farm industry.

He gets in a car made safer because of government regulations and travels toward his good job in a new manufacturing plant brought to his area through state and local government tax subsidies. He turns on the radio as he commutes and nods his head in agreement when a demagogue uses the public property of the airwaves to exercise a right to speak freely to vaguely condemn the governmental system that protects that right. But the shrill chatter soon wafts into the background as the young man drives down a smooth publicly funded highway, crosses a sturdy publicly funded bridge and sees a river made clean by environmental protection laws, daydreaming of taking a son there to fish some day. He arrives at his job, leans back into his leather office chair with a feeling of contentment, and imagines that he gained his position in life all by himself.

This person has an inaccurate perspective. He is not the autonomous mythical creature called the "self-made man," nor will he ever be. He is merely one of millions of citizens who have received the benefits of corporate American society just as surely as has the poor person on public support.

America has many parts, but we are one body. We are many peoples, but we are one indivisible nation. When one part of our society, or even one citizen in our society, suffers economic need that is disconnected from a lack of effort, all of us are hurt. We all lose when one is lost.

2. An Honest Living Wage

Freedom from want cannot practically be defined in terms of "daily bread." Although a famine victim or resident of a third-world country may well be satisfied with today's meal, an American citizen demands and deserves more. Freedom from want requires national confidence that diligently performing honest work will yield the following in excess of daily food, for one's self and family: shelter; medical care; transportation; and education. We should also be able to agree that we want our people to have children and raise them to be good citizens. Otherwise, our free society will die.

Thus, the amount of an honest day's wage for an honest day's work, an honest living wage, should also be sufficient to sustain young children. How else can a single parent persist in working? And for those children in households with both parents, how can the additional advantages of having both parents, such as a secure nurturing presence maintained in the home and parental involvement in school, arise if wages are so low that both parents must work full-time to meet basic needs? It should not require the full-time employment of both parents to support a modest family in America.

The Entitlement to Presumed Diligence

The pay due for unskilled entry-level work must be the threshold for consideration of a legitimate subsistence wage. The society providing for an honest living wage also has a right to presume honest diligence. Thus, the floor for basic wages should be established based on 60 hours a week rather than 40. While this is a longer week than most Americans work, particularly at the physically demanding work which is usually associated with unskilled labor, we should follow the adage that one who wants to make it, and proves so by diligence, should be able to do so. The 60-hour base calculation week also reflects a model allowing for one full-time worker and one part-time worker in a two-parent family to maintain itself financially. People may choose to raise children outside of the confines of marriage. But society has no obligation to financially endorse that decision.

Consider the minimal monthly needs of a family of four. Rent or a small mortgage will be at least $800. Food will be at least $400. Utilities will be at least $200. Adequate medical insurance will likely be at least $600. Transportation will be at least $300. Clothing will be at least $100. Child-care will be at least $200. The subtotal is $2600. Various taxes and miscellaneous items will add enough to take the total to at least $3000.

With basic needs of at least $3000 per month, calculation of a subsistence wage for a 240 hour work month (based on 60 hours a week) is simple: it comes to $12.50 per hour. Thus, the current minimum wage of $5.15 per hour would need to be more than doubled to provide the money legitimately needed for subsistence living. Receipt of at least an honest living wage for a full day's work is the necessary first step toward establishment of freedom from want. It would be a reasonable trade-off to have a lower base wage for those under 18 if a truly livable adult wage floor was put in place.

Opposition to an Honest Living Wage

Any mention of establishing an honest wage floor brings howls of despair from some employers. However, the fact is that it is already being more than paid in the form of numerous public support avenues.

Living above mere subsistence is available to the majority in our nation. However, many of our citizens of limited skills and educations, or those who have lost jobs through no fault of their own, are denied the opportunity to gain it through work. The work that they are qualified to perform does not pay an honest living wage. This situation gives rise to resentment from the taxpayers toward those who are not working to support themselves at the same time that it undermines the habit of work for many. It is shameful that 60 hours of work per week in the most prosperous and liberated nation in the history of the earth can be insufficient to provide basic subsistence for a small family.

The Illusion of Action

Ongoing welfare reforms calling for a set time of benefit entitlement during which job training or searching can be performed before termination of benefits cannot work effectively unless combined with an honest national wage floor. Many of those terminated from assistance will not have work available at their skill levels from which they can earn a subsistence living.

Some people envision an ideal world in which volunteerism and church organizations can consistently care for America's needy. I can also speak from experience on the church support issue. I was diagnosed with aplastic anemia (bone marrow failure) in 1984 that would have been fatal without a bone marrow transplant. Thankfully, health insurance was there through my employer to cover it. But I did not have the additional money for airfare to take me from my North Carolina home to Seattle for the procedure, much less to provide for my minor brother donor or our mother to stay with him while I was in a sterile "bubble" for a month.

My church was **WONDERFUL**. It gave me some $11,000.00 over about a 5-month period following my admission to the hospital, raising it by car washes and other events, as well as from giving straight from the members' pockets. This money prevented extreme financial hardship, bridging me over until I could secure other means of support during the 14 months of recovery time before I was able to return to work.

My personal situation could not have worked out better, and I will always hold those good people that helped me so much when I could not help myself in the fondest regard. But everyone does not have the sources of support that I had. Those not in church have the same needs as those that are. I expect that many of those that advocate that the poor should be mainly looked after by private sources have never been in a situation like that themselves. They may imagine that they are immune to or above or beyond such troubles; and I sincerely hope that they can persist in this illusion. But many have learned, as I did, that prosperity and strength can change to poverty and weakness in a flash, often through no fault of our own.

They also do not seem to understand that the attention span of people concerning any one issue or person is usually only a few months. Other matters arise. Other people get sick or have other hardships. But the needs of those already in trouble may carry on month after month. It would be cruel to subject the needy to the status of permanently soliciting for continuing attention. Our society has matured beyond this.

A Better Way

It would be far less financially and socially expensive for society to directly subsidize the wages of unskilled labor, bringing them up to an honest living wage level, than to continue on the current course of paying more than the full price for subsistence through multiple and changing sources with their associated overhead. We have work enough that needs to be done for all of the citizenry to be gainfully occupied. Folding the money from numerous support avenues into providing work, and leaving it to the people to pay for their own housing, child-care, and such, would greatly benefit the entire social structure. This would not be workfare. It would simply be work that is fair and honest.

Any additional public costs resulting from paying workers an honest living wage would be more than offset by the solutions provided for several of the most troubling matters that have long hindered us.

It would raise general wage rates by forcing competition for unskilled labor. Nevertheless, inflationary pressure may be negligible. As basic economics tells us, inflation results from increased numbers of dollars competing for the right to purchase a more slowly increasing quantity of goods. The number of dollars would not necessarily be increased. Money formerly paid for existence would then be paid for exertion. In fact, it could conceivably result in reduced public spending. Taxes deducted from the pay earned would partially offset the cost of providing the pay. There could potentially be downward pressure on general prices as new workers provide new goods and services and thereby gain more opportunity to bargain for housing and other products.

Businesses would be encouraged by the competition for labor to join into purchasing associations to provide access to health care coverage at the lowest group rates to prospective employees. This would cause pressure for reductions in administrative costs that would lower insurance rates for all. Insurance companies would compensate for lost revenues from reduced premiums by the receipt of new premiums from new customers.

Additionally allowing health care providers a streamlined legal avenue to wage garnishment for uninsured and unpaid medical bills at a rate substantially above a worker's standard group insurance rate would also lead to voluntary insurance purchasing by individuals who now ride freely on the backs of the insured. The new premiums paid and the recovery of payment by providers would further lower rates for all.

Generally lowered insurance costs and the transfer of the burden of insuring the able-bodied poor from government to individual workers would translate into many billions of dollars made available to reduce government borrowing, interest payments and taxes. We would thus move toward efficient national health care while contracting the size of government.

Current conditions result in constant bickering over benefits for illegal aliens. If the federal government acted as last resort employer, its foreign policy and immigration control responsibilities under the Constitution could allow a legally defensible framework for limiting employment under the system to citizens. Thus, the lure of the "land of plenty" for those unwilling to carry their own economic weight would be reduced, as would the unfortunate growing resentment toward all immigrants, even those who have become citizens.

Crime-ridden public housing projects would become a thing of the past. Able-bodied people would be free to live wherever they could afford to pay to live, with many of the lowest housing costs available in rural areas where children could more safely play.

The quality of inner city schools would be likely to increase due to a decreased number of students, resulting from parents moving to lower cost rural areas. The quality of rural schools would be likely to increase because of the addition of new taxpayers.

Homelessness, panhandling and crime related to poverty would be eradicated. Energy expended on work would not be available for mischief. The extent to which these symptoms remained would be without excuse, allowing citizens and government to equitably respond to them without emotionalism.

The sweat of parents would lead to their children's support. Most students would see school as a favorable alternative to beginning the responsibility of full-time work to support a child. Parents under the age of 18 may be considered too young to enter such a work system but should be fully responsible for their natural support obligations once reaching that age. Situations with both parents under-aged and unable to support their own children would result in the children either being supported by their own relatives or friends.

These friends could include churches and private charities. Providing part of the in-home support for some of the few children that would be born to two children under the age of eighteen, only until one parent reached eighteen, would constitute a reasonable and manageable portion of social responsibility for such institutions, particularly in light of the shared participation in savings and contributions that they would experience due to the introduction of a non-negotiable work requirement. It would also encourage these organizations to work in closer partnership with parents and young people to prevent conception of children before they can be afforded.

Young adults who wished to gain a high school education, or those having graduated high school who wanted further education, could get it on their own time, after making arrangements for the care of their own children through their own work, like countless other diligent Americans have done. At any rate, the presumed societal obligation toward child support outside of the context of providing work at an honest living wage would be essentially terminated.

True welfare reform should virtually eliminate the concept of welfare from our society. It should replace welfare with a system of fair work that universally requires diligence and rewards effort at least with sufficient wages to live on. It should eliminate any generally presumed societal obligation for indigent support. And it should presumptively rely on private sector initiatives for employment and health insurance.

Such a system would solve the true entitlement crisis of America, the resentment of taxpayers over unmerited support. The people paying for support by wages would see and experience tangible benefits of the support, in cleaner and safer streets and sturdier families. And those receiving the increased wages would be doing honest work and paying taxes, becoming full partners in our shared prosperity.

The truth set out in the Genesis account still stands: people <u>need</u> a garden to till. There is enough work and productivity in this great nation for all to have one.

3. Free Trade

Any consideration of American wages is incomplete without a consideration of international wages. Many low skilled jobs that Americans used to perform have gone to other countries. The trend has recently begun to move into higher skilled occupations. The resulting collapse of the wage floor in our economic house has caused downward pressure on wages above the floor for all but the most highly skilled workers, suppressing middle-class incomes and forcing ever-increasing dependence on two full-time wage earners in a household. This has negatively impacted home life and pushed many families toward desperation.

The Temptation for Tariffs

Some contend that maintenance and raising of low skilled wage rates for Americans can be arrived at by tariffs on imported goods. However, the costs of this approach are enormous. As factories that have moved to other nations, such as Mexico, move back here to avoid our tariffs, the pressure of illegal aliens seeking to cross our southern borders for work will increase beyond the current high levels. Furthermore, elements of capital and labor in a few industries will have enhanced opportunities for profiteering and unreasonable demands.

We should not forget that it took the threat of Japanese and European imports to encourage American automakers to shift toward fuel efficiency and quality. The pressure of competition has even resulted in sporadic cooperation among the major auto manufacturers to work towards further increases in gas mileage and production of electric cars and hydrogen fuel cells.

Achievement of such developments could help to free us from entanglements with totalitarian and unstable governments in oil producing nations that have hindered our national progress for decades. These efforts would not be underway without the presence in our market of imported cars from nations that pay higher gasoline bills than we do.

Under a tariff focused system, resentment will be quick from a public forced to pay rising prices for goods of possibly decreasing quality under threats of contrived shortages and frequent strikes. Furthermore, any increase in wages arrived at from tariffs will be an illusion since it will be devoured by an inflationary spiral generated by the protected industries that will always stay one step ahead of this year's wage.

An Open Markets Strategy

The primary alternative to a tariff system has traditionally been to seek to open the markets of other nations rather than closing our own. This approach seems to make particularly good sense when we consider that the United States' population, even as it approaches 300 million in 2004, represents less than one-twentieth of a world population exceeding six billion. Thus, some ninety-five percent of potential customers live outside of our country.

Most of the world is too poor to buy our goods, other than perhaps agricultural products. However, even if only ten percent of the rest of the world (600 million) possesses the wealth to take advantage of the full range of goods that we produce, the market available to American goods would be significantly increased if trade barriers between our various national markets were eliminated.

The North American Free Trade Agreement (NAFTA), passed near the end of 1993, followed the open markets strategy by establishing a protocol for essentially tariff-free trading among the markets of the United States, Canada and Mexico. For about one year after passage of the agreement, trade between the United States and Mexico, including imports and exports on both sides of the border, markedly increased, allowing the proponents of the agreement to bask in their apparent correctness. However, reality arrived while we were on the way to continental free trade bliss. The Mexican economy, a harsh mix of haves and have-nots supported by a government that historically had been very corrupt, and which was also destabilized by assassinations and a near civil war, began to falter by late 1994. The Mexican currency plummeted against the American dollar.

These factors caused Mexicans to be even more unable to buy our goods, whether in Mexico or in American border towns, and prompted a new flood of illegal immigrants to cross our southern border in search of work or other means of subsistence. The race of American businesses to Mexican locations was slowed because of fears of instability rather than lowered tariffs. And the United States government was compelled by its new marriage to comply with the duty of support by cobble-stoning a multi-billion dollar international loan package. Thus, the glowing expectations were stained after only a year.

The General Agreement on Tariffs and Trade (GATT) and, subsequently, the World Trade Organization (WTO), have had the potential for the same effects, both good and bad, in a multiplied fashion. Reduction in worldwide tariffs could have the same result as a massive international tax cut, with a large part of the benefit coming to the United States since we produce so much so efficiently. Similarly, political decisions made a half-world away could negatively affect our own lives, without us having leverage akin to our power to potentially control mass illegal immigration like we have with Mexico.

International trade agreements reveal the two-edged sword presented by an open markets strategy. Shared prosperity can swiftly change to shared hardship, with limited political control within our borders over unwise policies adopted in foreign lands that may lead to hardships here.

The Best Choice Among Alternatives

Even so, we should acknowledge that the potential for good existing by way of an open markets strategy is superior to the lack of potential long-term benefits available under a high tariff protectionist strategy. Emphasizing free trade also provides an inherent benefit unavailable under a tariff strategy that can help to support establishment of an honest living wage. International trade causes increases in transportation-related jobs due to the increase in goods shipped across national borders from all directions. Jobs building, operating, loading, unloading and maintaining trucks and ships and trains, jobs in highway and rail construction and maintenance, jobs in motel and food services, are all created by trade between nations.

It is no coincidence that many of the world's most wealthy people made their fortunes in transportation-related industries such as shipping and petroleum. Nor is it a coincidence that Great Britain, a small island nation, became a world power due to its strong navy and resulting ability to control shipping lanes and resource allocation. History has shown that transportation and trade provide sound roads to increased national wealth, even considering the risks involved. Increased trade will allow port cities which previously relied upon military installations for economic stability to be more prosperous in a future when their harbors are filled with privately financed ships of trade rather than tax-financed ships of war.

However, the world obviously remains a dangerous place where military prowess is a necessity. We must not fall into the trap of worshipping a false god of free trade, believing as we see our people put out of work, some of our industries decimated and our national security possibly threatened that The Almighty Market Will Provide.

No matter how effectively our trade arrangements may grow, we must maintain a base level of strategic industry in areas such as steel, motor vehicles, computer components and others necessary to wage war with when we must. Such industries must maintain strategic prosperity even if heavy subsidization is required, and even if our trading partners disagree. The complaints of other nations that have not opened their own markets to the extent that we have already opened ours should fall on deaf ears.

Phases of Trade

Now after more than a decade of increasingly free trade, we have not seen any increase in U.S. manufacturing jobs. In fact, we have seen a hastening decimation of American manufacturing from coast to coast and north to south. This is quite long enough to have continued at the experiment as we have, and way too long for our fellow citizens that have lost their jobs and standards of living in its wake. Citizens of other countries with standards of living similar to those enjoyed by our own people have come under similar pressures.

More recently, Americans are awakening to the fact that the people performing manufacturing jobs do not stand alone in having their livelihoods threatened. Service and professional jobs, from those in call centers to highly skilled ones in engineering, medicine and software functions, have begun to be relocated. Some of the countries that the jobs are being relocated to have populations large enough to absorb every U.S. occupation not tied to the land, and have wage rates so low as to create cost savings that greatly exceed the cost of shipping back into the American market. This is especially so when products are increasingly taking the shape of communications and electronic transactions that can be undertaken at virtually no cost.

Even those countries that previously enjoyed the boon of relocated industry have found the advantages short-lived. Mexico and Eastern European nations have recently begun to see that they were only way stations in a race to the lowest wages that ends in Asia, as their new manufacturing businesses have already begun to relocate.

This is obviously a situation that we, and others similarly situated, cannot allow to continue. It appears that we need to accept that international trade and tariff agreements should be re-negotiated. And, as in all negotiations, we must be willing to walk away from them if we cannot achieve a result that terminates the mass subsidization of jobs for people in other countries from the pockets and lives of our own. Price savings resulting from lower international wages will be fool's gold if they are obtained at the expense of our own neighbors.

However, we need not deteriorate into confrontational and accusatory trading relationships with Asian countries that are our national neighbors on this small planet. Taking the longer view, we can see that lowering tariffs was the first of a multi-phase process of international trade development. Shifting low skilled manufacturing labor costs to less expensive forums was merely a second phase, and not the terminal phase that the current, outdated, international trade protocols seem to imply. The third phase, shifting jobs that include higher skilled manufacturing and white-collar jobs to the least expensive forums, is where we now find ourselves.

Rather than engendering panic and reaction, this calls for realistic negotiations to further the interests of all parties to reach fourth and subsequent phases that yield net benefit to all participants. We have primary interests in secure and improving economic circumstances for our own people, secondary interests in low prices and tertiary interests in the standards of living in other countries. The Asian countries supplying the less expensive labor pools have their own hierarchy of interests in maintaining access to the markets of the more developed nations in order to maintain the economic advancements of their own peoples that have been accelerated by access to those markets. There is a net economic benefit to the world that occurs when goods are produced in the most efficient locations, and the money from that benefit flows somewhere. It needs to flow broadly and equitably rather than narrowly.

It may be that higher tax rates on domestic companies that create their goods abroad and reintroduce them into the American market are called for. Some will say that the companies will merely pass the costs along to the consumers, which is true enough. However, in doing so the companies will merely be selling the good for the truer value, rather than at values subsidized by Americans through job loss and taxation. And, when true and unsubsidized prices are charged, manufacturing will relocate back to productive American workers.

Creative international negotiations that focus on mutual interests will certainly be necessary to make sure that Americans receive our fair share of the benefit of international trade. One alternative may be a sort of international progress pool whereby market access is valued for reimbursement to countries at an agreed rate. The third phase relocation of jobs from Mexico and Eastern Europe to Asia is now creating an international political context where more than just the U.S. and other traditionally prosperous countries may be interested in such a system adjustment. In any case, creative negotiations carried out within the context of what we have all learned from past experience can provide a smooth transition to a better way for all.

International trade need not undermine our commitment to an honest living wage. In fact, it can help us to more efficiently establish it. And, despite the risks associated with free trade, it is a superior system to one based on pessimistic trade protectionism.

However, free trade is not a national religion. We are under no obligations to market theories that would require us to compromise our national security or our corporate well being. To analogize from the words of Jesus Christ concerning the Sabbath Day, the market was made for man, not man for the market.

The market is simply a tool, like a hammer or saw, with a purpose of allowing exchanges. It can be used to build or allowed to destroy. We have a corporate right to demand that it only be used within our borders to build and contribute to our shared national prosperity.

4. The Gift of Life

We should consider how to gain the full world's participation while pursuing the path to our own prosperity. Africa, the cradle of life from which the ancestors of black citizens were brought to America, is haunted by the threat of repeated famine. One of those famines contributed to the troublesome American and United Nations relief efforts in Somalia in the early 1990s.

The greatest gift that America could provide for Africa, once all Americans are allowed the dignity of a livable day's wage for an honest day's work, would be to end African famine, at least as it results directly from weather patterns, by developing more inexpensive means of mass desalinization of ocean water. Research toward this end would allow us to learn to better provide for the growing water needs of our own southwestern cities and farms as well as other areas periodically afflicted by drought. We would also reduce the potential for future interventions on the African continent that have been emotionally inspired by the sight of starving people.

Much of the African continent will not be able to participate in international trade to a significant extent until the cycle of famine is banished. People who are threatened with starvation are unconcerned with the finer things of life.

Once the African nations are full trading partners, and the Russians and Chinese and peoples of the Middle East, the tri-polar prosperity that is now mainly enjoyed by North America, Europe and some of the Asian Pacific nations can spread to the full circle of the globe. Such enhanced economic interaction will reduce temptation for aggression as more nations participate in the advantages of trade over the devastation of war.

5. Other Areas of Research Emphasis

There are at least three other key areas in which our research should be centered to continue the march toward freedom from want. The first is health, the second is energy and the third is environment.

AIDS is the latest scourge to devastate Africa. Neither the United States nor the international community can dictate the self-care necessary to bring this menace under control. However, we have rightly committed to help how we can, and should certainly follow through with medicinal support, especially with inexpensive remedies that can keep newborns from contracting the disease from their mothers.

We should also continue to encourage active corporate support through government for research for other major diseases. Many cures and methods to alleviate human suffering have been developed by way of government-financed research. We should not be "penny-wise and pound-foolish" by curtailing such research because of budget pressures. The potential benefits to future generations are too great to turn back in this area.

Public health research is an area that is very personally near and dear to me. I am very aware that medical research funding for bone marrow transplantation is what saved my life after a diagnosis of lethal aplastic anemia in 1984. The process was not nearly so widespread then as now, having only been performed for a decade or so. At least there was some human history of the procedure when I had it. One volunteer at the medical center where I was treated, whose son had undergone the process before, told of only being able to learn what the success rate had been with the dogs.

A necessary part of the research process for bone marrow transplantation and most other life-saving medical procedures involves using hundreds of animals for experimentation before the first attempt can be made on a human. I marvel at people that interfere with use of animals for medical experimentation, and can only conclude that they have been fortunate enough to not have to depend on the results of the research to save their own lives or those of people that they love. Once again, the educating forces of perspective and empathy seem to be absent. Yes, the animals should be treated as humanely as possible, but the research should certainly continue, and at as fast a rate as we can reasonably support.

Our national self-interest also directs that short-term energy research should be focused upon development of cost effective forms of electric batteries and hydrogen cells for cars. Traveling city streets and country highways with no engine noise and no exhaust would greatly improve our breathing, hearing and general health.

Until this form of transportation is practical, we need sufficient oil supplies that are as disconnected from Middle Eastern volatility as possible. Thus, Alaskan oil exploration and extraction should be expanded, with the utmost care and caution. We cannot reasonably ignore any potential source of oil when Middle Eastern sources seem to always have us entangled in some sort of expensive trouble. It would be well worth greatly subsidizing high cost domestic extractions if we could get enough oil from them to ease foreign dependence.

The sad truth is that we have engaged in a bipartisan strategy of trading weapons for oil since the early 1980s to ensure cheap gas prices. Conservation and energy independence initiatives have slowed in return. It would make for an interesting economic study to estimate our true cost for a gallon of gas, with international subsidies and costs of war included.

Of course, the true cost in money, no matter how large, would not begin to calculate the loss of life and national prestige that we have suffered as a direct result of our continuing entanglement in the incessantly volatile Middle East. And the entanglement just gets deeper and more expensive year by year, with our alternative courses of action always handicapped by dependence on the region's oil. We should do all that we can to free ourselves of this addicting entrapment. Indeed, showing that we are moving in the direction of energy freedom is the best way that we can exercise leverage there for positive ends as those controlling the oil see a formerly dependable cash cow slipping away to graze in another pasture. This method may be more effective than trying to maintain military and diplomatic influence over a huge area with millions of hostile people half a world away.

The environment should also continue to be a focus of government-financed research. This area impacts on all others. An unclean and dangerous environment detracts from our health, and the primary causes of environmental deterioration result from the forms of energy that we use. Continued development of methods of energy creation by clean waste incineration can help in this area, as may continued research into electric vehicles and even nuclear fusion. We should also persist in funding research for other energy sources such as solar and wind power.

Some influential voices deride the extensive body of evidence from otherwise well-regarded scientists concerning global warming and climate change from burning fossil fuels. Some similarly discount the damage we are doing to the oceans, even when it is increasingly well documented that areas once teaming with fish are thinning out and catches are becoming smaller. What will these people say when the evidence becomes even more irrefutable but the time has passed when we can any longer do anything about it? Many of us will ask ourselves why we listened to them. Such thinking seems akin to that of our ancestors that decimated the buffalo herds by using the animals for target practice. Most of us now consider the people that did that to have been incredibly wasteful and foolish, even primitive. None of us want future Americans to think the same of us.

We need to lead the world, rather than lag it, on environmental protections and efficient energy use. There is no other country that can do it besides us, and it is truly one of our core international duties and responsibilities, for our own benefit more than for that of others.

All of this research will involve large expenditures, with no profit-making potential for at least several years. In the area of our funding of projects that can benefit all of humankind for today and the remainder of history, there is no factor that has a more limiting impact on establishing freedom from want than government debt. Money spent on interest on the debt cannot be spent in other needed areas.

6. The Debt and Taxation

In discussing the debt of the United States government, we need to understand some basics. First, the difference between the terms deficit, debt, and balanced budget should be clear.

The budget deficit is the amount in one year by which government spending exceeds the money that comes into the government, mostly from taxes. The debt is the total amount owed, resulting from years of deficit spending. A balanced budget results when the government spends no more money in a year than it brings in.

The federal government of the United States has deficits and debt separate from the governments of the states, counties, and cities. The federal government measures its deficits on the basis of a fiscal, or accounting, year that runs from October 1 through the following September 30.

The federal deficit for fiscal year 1995 (October 1, 1994, through September 30, 1995) was about $160 billion. This was about half the amount of interest ($320 billion) paid on the total debt of nearly $5 trillion at the time. The deficit for 2004 is likely to exceed $400 billion, and the total debt is now at about $7 trillion ($7,000,000,000,000). Thus, we have added another $2 trillion, increasing the debt by 40 percent, in only the past decade. The nation's total debt through 204 years of history stood at about $1 trillion in 1980. So, in just 24 years, just over a tenth of the nation's history, we have multiplied our debt by 7 times.

Just How Big Is It?

Reducing the numbers involved into more understandable portions is essential to understanding the size of the debt. Most of us consider a millionaire to be quite well off. A million dollars would last for twenty years if spent at a rate of $50,000 per year. A million is a thousand thousand.

A billion is one thousand million. People who have accumulated a billion dollars are among the richest on earth. A person could spend $50 million dollars per year for twenty years before exhausting $1 billion. The 1995 federal deficit of $160 billion amounted to federal government borrowing of almost $1/2 billion dollars every day of the year. As of 2004, daily borrowing has exceeded $1 billion.

A trillion is one thousand billion. It would require that the federal government spend $100 billion dollars per year less than it takes in to retire $1 trillion in debt over ten years. The total federal debt, at about $7 trillion, would thus require 70 years to retire with persistent annual budget surpluses of $100 billion. The population of the whole world is somewhere between 6 and 7 billion. That means that the American government now owes the equivalent of about $1000 for every living human on earth.

Let's look at the debt in some other ways that may not seem so overwhelming. The deficit for 2004 will probably exceed $400 billion. The current population of the United States approaches 300 million. Dividing the $400 billion deficit by the population equals about $1300 of new borrowing per person for the year, about $3.50 a day. Considering that about 140 million pay income taxes, the added debt per taxpayer this year is about $2800, $7.70 a day. The total debt per person is about $23,000, and per taxpayer about $50,000.

The U.S. population grew from about 220 million in 1980 to its current level approaching 300 million. With the total national debt multiplied by 7 times, from $1 trillion to $7 trillion over the same 24 years, the per-household share of the debt has risen considerably. Some argue that increasing debt relative to population to such a degree over such a short period of time threatens the growth in our general standard of living.

Yet, these numbers do not seem so daunting when many of our middle-class families routinely carry home-loan debt above $200,000, and when it is not unusual for student loan debt to exceed $100,000. With our annual national economy at well over $10 trillion, a $7 trillion debt is manageable. Most of us would consider an individual with a $100,000 income and $70,000 of debt to cover a fine home, great transportation and superb medical care very well off. This would be the individual analogous to our country.

The national debt certainly generates interest payments that take money from important projects into which many Americans feel more should be placed, such as crime control, education and medical research. The debt has similarly reduced money available to go to state and city governments, causing higher state and local income taxes, sales taxes and property taxes.

We need to test our debt spending by asking whether it will leave posterity sufficient benefit to make paying it back worthwhile, for the future earners will be the ones with its burden. Will today's American children receive any advantage from the national debt created by their parents and grandparents? The answer is very clearly still yes. We have used it to arm and sustain ourselves in the face of military and economic threats. But, some may say that the problem with debt management has been an increasing inefficiency over time.

Less Bang for the Buck?

The current national debt has arisen almost completely since the 1920s. It totaled about $20 billion when Franklin Roosevelt took office in 1932 in the midst of the Great Depression. After several years of necessary borrowing to get the people of our nation through the economic emergency, the total debt was still only about $50 billion by 1940. Calculating $30 billion borrowed for 8 years of the Great Depression out at 3 percent inflation from 1940 through 2004 translates to about $200 billion ($30 \times (1.03)^{64} = 199$), about half of the $400 billion projected for 2004.

From 1940 to 1947, the years during and immediately after World War II, the total debt grew from about $50 billion to about $250 billion, multiplying by about five times. Calculating $200 billion of debt spending used to fight powerful German and Japanese enemies that threatened our national existence out at 3 percent inflation through 2004 translates to just over $1 trillion ($200 \times (1.03)^{57} = 1078$), about 2 ½ times the debt we are accumulating in 2004. Yes, the 9/11 Tragedies and the mild recession that reached its depth 3 years ago were very negative economic events, and we now have two ongoing military actions in Iraq and Afghanistan against enemies that should be hopelessly overmatched. But does it make sense that these events can justify borrowing twice as much in one year as we did to get through 8 years of the Great Depression, or almost half as much in one year as we borrowed to fight World War II?

We had to deal with the international Communist threat, primarily from the Soviet Union, after World War II. One of our first major efforts on that front was the Marshall Plan, a huge economic rebuilding of our vanquished German and Japanese enemies. With the Marshall Plan investment, we created a form of economic barrier to go along with the military containment policy relative to the Soviet Union, by helping two economically thriving democracies to exist at the borders of the Soviet bloc.

The $12 billion spent under the Marshall Plan over more than a dozen years through its conclusion in the early 1960s translates to about $40 billion in today's dollars (12 x $(1.03)^{40}$ = 39). $20 billion of the 2004 debt can be attributed to new spending resulting from the first year's rebuilding installment sent into Iraq. Should we spend half as much in a year to try to develop a friendly Iraqi democracy as we did over more than a decade to fund the Marshall Plan?

Military containment of the Soviet Communist system since the end of World War II has been the leading source of our debt spending. The containment policy led to a long, bloody and complicated war in Vietnam, and surrogate face-offs in dozens of other countries, all battles in the Cold War. Contrary to some rhetoric, Iraq is no Vietnam. This is not because of the disparity in American casualties. After all, Vietnam did not start out with 58,000 American soldiers dead. At one point less than 1000 Americans had died there also. The difference lies in the fact that there is no large economic force available to credibly fund the Iraqi insurgents against what we can bring to bear, as there was during the Cold War and Vietnam through Soviet military spending.

Let's consider one more example. The 2004 deficit will bring the total new debt in the last 5 years to nearly $1 trillion. To keep things simple, let's equally divide the reasons justifying it, with $500 billion for the 9/11 Tragedies and war, and $500 billion for economic stimulus. Let's further do away with finger-pointing about lost manufacturing jobs over the past several years and say that we started 2004 on a historically equal footing, and that the jobs created through $1/2 trillion of debt stimulus will finally come to fruition this year, with the average amount of jobs generated for 12 full months very impressive, at about the level of the 300,000 generated during March, April and May of 2004, for 3.6 million new jobs. If this optimistic scenario plays out for the full 12 months of 2004, dividing the $500 billion by 3.6 million will equal over $130,000 per job. This level of spending to create a military job may make sense, considering the expensive equipment and training involved, and the fact that all military jobs have the incalculable benefit of directly contributing to our nation's security. But,

$130,000 a job for average civilian jobs begs the question of whether that is efficient job creation.

The Holy Bible proclaims itself to be for our instruction. Let's go back to the Hebrew Bible to consider the story of Joseph. How did he save Egypt? He followed a simple plan, raising taxes during the 7 "fat years" of plenty and saving the surplus to be used in the 7 "lean years" of need. It was a good thing for the children of Israel that they had Joseph in charge. They would have been starved away had he seen the fat years as an opportunity to let the good times roll.

Of course, we do not have the benefit of Joseph's inspired dream interpretations to be able to know when our "fat years" and "lean years" are coming. But, we can get a fair idea of historic trends from stock markets and business cycles. The lean years of the Great Depression consumed the last of the 1920s and all of the 1930s, which ended with the Dow Jones Industrial Average at about 100. General economic expansion multiplied the Dow by 10, to about 1000, over the next 20 years, from 1940-60. These economically fat years were followed by an equal period of 20 years, from 1960-80, when the Dow struggled to hold 1000. We just emerged in 2000 from another cycle of 20 fat years when the Dow multiplied by 10 again, from 1000 to over 10,000. And it has again struggled to hold 10,000 since 2000. If we are now in another cycle of 20 lean years, then we have 16 more to go. And we did not save during the fat years to prepare for the lean. Rather, we decided to consume the surplus. And, if we are now in another prolonged period of relative economic doldrums, then we can reasonably expect that it will take relatively greater debt to yield appropriate economic benefit.

Some suggest that government spending will always simply increase to outpace new revenues. But the facts do not support this opinion. Democrats controlled the Congress from 1948 until 1980, with Republicans and Democrats exactly splitting time in the Presidency at 16 years each, but did not generate deficit spending at anywhere near the levels that have existed since 1981. Tax and spending changes passed with bipartisan support in the Congress since that year have yielded the changed debt picture, for better or for worse.

A Better Risk

Any consideration of a balanced budget constitutional amendment to alter the debt should be very warily made. We should remember that some of our most important debt spending did not receive 60 percent votes of support in both houses of Congress, as most balanced budget amendment proposals would require.

It is irrelevant that most state government constitutions require operation under a balanced budget. States do not have the responsibility of financing the national defense. A bad year with a state budget causes pain enough, resulting in angry and deprived people for a few months. A bad budget year for the federal government, in the event that 41 percent of the Congress is short sighted and makes a wrong decision, could potentially damage American democracy.

Such a risk is too great to take. Thus, we need to reject the idea of a federal constitutional balanced budget amendment as a solution and, instead, concentrate our energies on reasonably, and patiently, institutionalizing budget responsibility. Doing so can even allow us to banish the borrow and pay-down cycle that we have repeated over the decades.

Both major party candidates contending for the 2004 Presidential election have pledged to halve the annual deficit by 2008, to bring it to about $200 billion. This is very doable and, with minor budgetary adjustments, it is easy to foresee a return to surplus by 2012, even if we are in another 20-year down cycle. Total debt will likely total about $9 trillion by that time, which should still be considerably smaller than the size of the annual national economy. Our leaders would be wise to resist the temptation to cut taxes upon a return to surplus and, rather, act to lock in a 50-50 system of pay-down and accumulation. Half of the surplus should go to eliminating the debt over the remainder of the century. The other half should go to a homes and highways fund to be loaned out at low interest to individuals and states to stimulate home ownership and infrastructure support, and for use during national emergencies.

Aside from the national security benefits, such a shift in priorities would yield great rewards in economic stimulus, as the money was spent and as future interest payments were foregone. Getting far ahead of the prolonged business cycle in this way would further help to smooth it out during future lean years.

Equal Rate Cuts?

The biggest deficits have resulted when large income tax rate cuts were combined with large spending increases, with bipartisan approval in the Congress. Although the associated tax cuts were approximately equal on a percentage basis for all citizens, a situation that seems fair at first glance, the cuts may have served to institutionalize an unfair division of the necessary economic labor of financing government.

The legitimate question has never been whether to tax. Rather, it has been how to tax most fairly, so that the financial burdens of government and public services are shared by as many as possible, without any particular group bearing an inordinate share of the expenses.

We answered the question of tax fairness for most of the twentieth century with a policy of progressive income taxation, taxing persons at higher rates as their incomes increased. Business owners who chose to incorporate were taxed in the same way, allowing their businesses to accept tax responsibility as individual persons in exchange for receiving the protection from financial and legal responsibilities that incorporation provides.

This system provided relative economic stability and a strengthening of the middle class within a context of reasonably limited government borrowing. Business interests benefited from the expanded purchasing power of a growing middle class, and generated more capital despite higher rates of taxation on higher incomes.

Consider a case where a person with a taxable income of $40,000 paid 10% ($4000) in federal income taxes. His 25 percent tax cut would yield $1000 more over the course of a year. This is a nice bit of money to most people, but not what most could use to make more money with, particularly since it was probably dealt out over 26 or 52 paychecks at $20 to $40.

Should the modest earner have saved and invested it? Possibly. Did he? Probably not. The natural response of a modest wage-earner with an extra $20 per week in his pocket was to consume it for his own or his children's meals or shoes, or, in cases of exemplary discipline, upon a little extra spending at Christmas or during vacation. The modest earner, who struggles to meet the daily needs for himself and his family, seldom reaches the threshold of comfort necessary for systematic saving or investment. On the contrary, his constant spending on consumption represents the demand that drives the economy.

Consider the result of the same tax cut for a person earning $150,000 of taxable income per year. Had that person been paying about $25,000 in income taxes (17%) before such a cut, his net gain from a 25 percent tax cut would have been $6250, or about $120 per week, 6 times the amount received by the modest income worker, although his taxable income was less than 4 times higher, and his prior level of taxation, on a percentage basis, was less than 2 times higher. At that income level, consumption spending for lunches, cigarettes, Christmas presents and vacations have not likely been of serious concern for years.

Contrary to the modest earner, whose pay goes almost entirely to life's necessities, the natural response of the individual with the $150,000 income to receiving an extra $120 per week, or $480 per month, would be to invest it, creating more capital for himself over time. Thus, while people with higher incomes have gained more wealth under equal percentage rate cuts, those of modest incomes have done well if they held their economic ground against even moderate inflation.

Looking at it another way, the higher income earner still paid six times more taxes on his $150,000 income than did the modest earner on his $40,000 income, paying about $19,000 compared to $3000 after the equal percentage rate cuts. But the amount of money left over after the equal percentage reductions also yielded a greater increase in remaining income for the high earner than for the modest earner. The higher earner's remaining income, $125,000 (at total income taxes of $25,000) increased by about 5 percent, to $131,000. The increase in remaining income for the modest earner, on the other hand, was less than 3 percent, from $36,000 before the equal tax cut to $37,000 after.

Missed Metaphors

Cutting taxes at higher income levels has long been advocated as benefiting modest earners by strengthening businesses and providing jobs to which they can be hired. Opponents of this method have derided it as trickle-down economics for just as long.

The problem with this description is the substance chosen as the economic metaphor: water. If wealth were actually like water, tending to trickle down, then those at the top of the income scale would be hard pressed to retain it as economic gravity tended to pull it towards the poorest of the poor, who could soon expect to be wealthy.

With pay raises hard to come by, jobs hard to keep and progress slow in coming for the modest earner, this argument is not credible. The correct metaphor for wealth is not water: it is helium. Wealth will never flow down the economic scale of its own accord. It will always fly upward if barriers to its mobility are removed. Any monetary benefit bestowed down the income scale will either be motivated by getting the largest return for the smallest investment or by compulsion, such as by labor organization or through progressive taxation.

Consider the Great Depression of the 1920s and 1930s. There was no shortage of wealth in our country. America was still a rich country. But the money was coagulated at the top of the economic scale, unable to circulate. Increasingly progressive taxation, higher government spending (for World War II) and increased strength in organized labor renewed healthy circulation.

The percentage of total income taxes paid by high earners has increased with diminished progressivity in the tax code. But, it has not increased as fast as the total percentage of national income and wealth controlled at the top of the scale. And the size of the total economic pie has not grown fast enough for many citizens of modest incomes to hold their relative economic positions, much less make progress. As we approached the twenty-first century, the top one percent of American income earners controlled more than forty percent of total American wealth, the greatest percentage held at the top of the scale since the days of the Great Depression.

Some consider this a good thing, logically reasoning that big gainers are usually big risk-takers that have thereby earned the gains. Others of contrary persuasion have warned of doom and gloom over income disparity for years, and sometimes even seem almost disappointed that most of us continue to earn enough year by year to remain relatively content.

History teaches that extremism from either the left or right sides of the political spectrum yields equally oppressive results. And history also teaches that the wealth of a nation is its life's blood. Like the blood in a body, it must circulate to all parts. The privileged head cannot safely observe from a distance while a lack of circulation causes gangrene in the little toe. Infection will arise that will lead to spreading of the damage and loss of the foot, then the leg and then the life of the entire body. Therefore, those with the most have the most at stake in maintaining a healthy economy.

We have reached a time when salaries and winnings for athletes and other entertainers routinely reach many millions of dollars. Some executive compensation levels have gotten even more ridiculous. Having so few receive so much for so little does not provide the type of goal-setting compass that can benefit our society.

Citizens generally do not care to deny a person the opportunity to be paid whatever can be honestly had, which is millions for some. However, those not as skilled or fortunate should at least be able to expect that they will earn enough to live on for a full day of honest work, and that high earners will carry a fair share of the load of keeping the democracy operating that has allowed the advantage to be earned.

The Flat Tax

Replacing what remains of the progressive income tax with a flat tax to collect an equal percentage of tax on all incomes would amplify inequity. Consider the same earners as before, with taxable incomes of $40,000 and $150,000. Application of a true flat tax of 15 percent on the taxable incomes of each would result in

$6000 in taxation on the modest earner and $22,500 in taxation on the higher earner. The higher earner, who has long ago lost serious concern for items such as housing and food, would be taxed about the same as his earlier $25,000 at 17 percent. The modest earner, who spends nearly his entire income for the necessities of life, would get a substantial tax increase over his previous $4000 at 10 percent.

Flat tax supporters tout the supposed simplicity of the proposal, with its elimination of deductions, and usually promise a hearty exemption for modest income earners, ranging up to more than $40,000 under some proposals. Thus, the modest earner would have no income tax responsibilities with a $40,000 income exemption, and his take home pay would be increased by about 11 percent from the $36,000 that he had been taking home after $4000 of income taxes.

The $40,000 exemption would, of course, also apply to the individual with the $150,000 income, leaving his taxable income at $110,000. Applying a 15 percent flat rate to this income would generate $16,500 in tax revenue.

Such a policy would have to result in greater debt. The flat tax described, with a $40,000 income exemption, would reduce by over 30 percent the amount of taxes paid by the higher earner if he had previously been paying $25,000 in income taxes. Adding the lost revenue from the total lack of taxation on the modest earner, $4000, to the total decrease in taxation on the high earner, $8,500 ($25,000 less $16,500), equals $12,500 less going to the government, or a decrease in total tax collections from the two earners of 43 percent from the $29,000 that they would have paid.

The National Sales Tax

Some advocate replacing all income taxation with a consumption tax, or national sales tax. This would also shield higher earners and corporations from tax obligations. A federal sales tax approaching 20 percent will likely be required for revenues to approach required spending.

How many millions of citizens, whose modest incomes now only require modest taxation, would lose the ability to buy expensive items, such as new cars, because of new sales taxes? A 20 percent federal sales tax placed on a $20,000 car would raise its price by $4000 (the same amount as the prior annual income tax for the modest earner taxed at 10 percent) before addition of state and local sales taxes, to probably be financed over three to five years. Prices for other items would also be raised by 20 percent (with possible exceptions for groceries, medicines and housing), with credit purchases paid for over time.

For all items not paid for in cash, from automobiles to business lunches, from shoes to fertilizer to gasoline, we would be compelled by a consumption tax to pay interest to banks on the associated taxation. Thus, the honest modest earner would have his tax status reduced to that now reserved for late payers and tax cheats who must pay interest to the government on their delinquencies, with the tax cheat probably paying the government at a lower rate than would be paid to the banks.

Consider the impact on higher income and modest earners. The $150,000 earner would be free of his income tax obligation of $25,000 (17%), as would the $40,000 earner of his obligation of $4000 (10%). The purchase prices of both would be increased by 20 percent.

The modest earner was probably already spending nearly his entire after tax $36,000 just to make ends meet, and would likely have spent several thousand more if he'd had it. Even if we assume that $6000 spent on foods and medicines and $10,000 for housing will not be taxed, that leaves $24,000 that he would still spend with his income taxes eliminated. Multiplying this amount by 20 percent equals $4800 in national sales taxes that would be paid instead of $4000 in income taxes, a 20% tax increase.

Suppose our frugal modest earner did not need to borrow to comfortably make ends meet before the change, a circumstance that might allow him to invest the $4000 in income taxes saved. Also suppose that he could invest the saved income tax money at 10 percent. He could earn an extra $400 during the year after paying $4000 in national sales taxes on $20,000 of consumption spending. The modest earner who must borrow will have higher additional costs from federal sales taxation financed through banks at interest. Of course, those who now pay no income tax, because they have no taxable income, from the housewife on a budget to children with their allowances and money from mowing lawns and baby-sitting, will also pay the tax.

Contrary to the modest earner's need to spend nearly every dime on the necessities of life, the $150,000 earner is probably already investing $10,000 to $20,000 per year of his after tax $125,000. Thus, the $25,000 saved from income tax will be available to multiply a growing nest egg. But in the interest of tax fairness, assume that the higher earner will spend his entire $150,000 income, and that he will only spend the same $16,000 for nontaxable groceries, medicine and housing as his modest earning fellow-citizen. His $27,000 in total sales taxes paid will approximate his previous 17% income tax bill of $25,000. Living better, in a bigger house with better food and a healthy investment account, will reduce his taxes by reducing his taxable spending.

Big Business Bonanzas

Flat tax and consumption tax proposals usually also include elimination of corporate income taxes and capital gains taxes. Benefit could thus be gained under a flat tax by incorporation or translating pay from income to shares of corporate stock to thereby avoid any tax responsibility. Under a consumption tax, banks and finance companies receiving additional billions of dollars in interest from financed taxation on consumption borrowing would be free from paying taxes on the increase. And when selling shares of bank stock, with values increased due to the infusion of new cash, shareholders would be free from tax responsibility no matter how great the capital gains.

7. Deregulation

Deregulation has been near the top of the list of political discussion topics since Jimmy Carter began campaigning for the 1976 presidential election. He promised to reduce federal government agencies and rules just like he had done in Georgia. He delivered on the promise after his election by deregulating the air travel and truck transport industries.

Reducing government influence continues to be a powerful vote getter. After air travel and trucks, we determined that the savings and loan industry needed less government regulation so it could be more profitable. Later, we moved on to electricity and energy. These examples of deregulation have yielded government bailouts, scandals, lowered wages and dozens of bankruptcies in formerly stable industries. Savings and loan deregulation, in particular, resulted in a huge government subsidy to big banks that were able to buy savings and loan assets for pennies on the dollar. And, part of the scandal of Enron is closely connected to energy deregulation.

Reality has a strange way of shaking the tree of dogma to its roots. We rushed to place new regulations on stock trading that limited the use of high-speed computer transactions after the market crashed in October 1987. Higher regulatory hurdles with regard to responsibilities of corporate boards of directors, lawyers and mutual fund managers are still evolving following the subsequent round of business scandals and market collapse over a decade later.

We need to consider that all regulations were put into place for a reason, and examine the original reasoning behind the regulations before discarding them. This is especially true in cases where society has grown accustomed to operating under the regulations for many years.

Clearly outdated or counter-productive rules should be set aside. But we need to take heed that we do not impose a cure that is worse than the disease. We need not amputate the foot for an ingrown nail.

It is easy to discount the need for government regulations, such as environmental and food safety controls, when rivers no longer burn with toxic waste fires and food poisonings are rare. But the surest way to usher these and dozens of other menaces back into our society is to eviscerate the laws that did away with the threats in the first place.

8. Capital Organization

Money is primarily a transitional device by which we can obtain what we want. And one of the things that we all should want is capital, which can be broadly defined as control of means of production. The old saying that it takes money to make money is true, for it takes capital to make wealth.

Human ingenuity is a form of capital. One of the most basic forms of physical capital is land. Wealth can be repeatedly gained from land either by the growing of crops or from rent. Land is a form of capital that can produce wealth indefinitely if it is well managed. However, once technology has generated the inevitable shift from land-based occupations to industry and supporting services, as has increasingly been the case in our nation since the early part of the twentieth century, the primary form of physical capital becomes the means of industrial production by which we create the material things that we want. Contrary to land, this form of capital cannot rejuvenate itself if allowed to lie fallow. It requires a constant infusion of money.

Labor can certainly be a means of accumulating capital and wealth. Expanding the average wages of labor through educational advancement and increased productivity can speed the process. By thus providing additional creative opportunities for a broader range of citizens, society profits from those who may have previously been excluded. However, capital has an exponential effect upon the capacity for generation of wealth that labor cannot match.

Failing to understand this principle is the basic flaw of communist/socialist systems. By transferring societal anger from persons who used capital and trade as weapons of predation to the ideas of capital and trade, the proponents of such systems doom the people governed by them to chronic under-production and decreasing wealth. When a desire for military conquest was mingled with such an inherently self-defeating system, even a wealthy nation like the former Soviet Union had to eventually collapse under its own weight.

Contrary to the socialist model, the way to reach societal prosperity for all is not to place all physical capital, as if it were a dangerous beast, within the hands of the state for control and taming. The way to reach this goal is to create means by which more people can honestly attain capital, allowing all to be capitalists.

Besides creating the means for additional and more widely dispersed wealth, there is another key reason for encouraging wide access to capital growth by promoting education, small business creation and investment in ownership of company securities. In days gone past, labor organization in the form of unions contributed to balance in society to control the unscrupulous activities of capital predators. While this function has not totally disappeared, its power is diminished daily as new technologies take the place of repetitive labor functions previously performed by people.

Such technologies make possible the creation of a future of relative leisure in which the only labor performed will be in maintenance of machines, entertainment and skilled workmanship. However, once the power of the majority to influence capital activity by the withholding of labor evaporates, economic power outside the scope of intellectual property will be concentrated in physical capital. This will not be a pleasant situation if that capital is mainly controlled by unrestrained predatory personalities.

We already see the development of this situation in its early stages. Although the total economy of America continues to grow, the additional wealth created is increasingly siphoned toward a minority of the population. The general citizenry, on the other hand, is continually intimidated into doing more with less as the last vestiges of job security are stripped away from occupation after occupation. A nation that should be gradually developing into a land of contented artisans is, thus, being directed towards reduction to the status of depending upon the hand of kindness from others, some of them ill-disposed to grant it. Relocation of capital and jobs to lower wage markets in other countries is hastening the process.

There are at least three ways to reverse these negative trends. One is by extensive capital participation throughout the population. As was seen in the case of South African apartheid, the organized votes of corporate shareholders against doing business under that corrupt system caused disinvestment by corporate board members who were previously content to operate there, and they helped lead to the birth of democracy. This method can also be used here to provide constructive guidance to those who might otherwise be tempted toward predatory activities.

More accurate disclosure of and accounting for executive pay will be necessary to allow the development of true shareholder democracy. Perhaps the changes enacted in the wake of the Enron scandals will help us avoid other such incidents in the future. As in the electoral process for public office, the key to good decision making for voting shareholders is accurate and timely information.

A second way to encourage moderation is by extensive participation by the citizenry in the actual democratic process of voting for leaders who will, once elected, represent the interests of the majority. Campaign finance reform that reduces the emphasis on broadcasting will be necessary for this goal to be fully attained.

Thirdly, progressive income taxation for individuals and corporations should be preserved so that the majority will have a fair opportunity for capital accumulation. The vast population of the general American citizenry is neither morally nor politically compelled to allow the few to profit unduly at the expense of the many. Contrary to the vanquished and rightfully discredited communist system, ours generates sufficient value for high earners to maintain and improve their stations, and for the many to live in dignity.

FREEDOM FROM FEAR

Let's travel back in time, to long before our revolution in 1776. Let's go back before the time of Christ, before Moses, before Noah. As we arrive at our destination, the dawn of civilization, what do we see? There are primitive people deciding to dwell together in groups that increase in size over time, under established sets of rules, for purposes of community, commerce and protection from fear—fear of predatory beasts and predatory people. This ancient urge, to be free from fear, is a primary reason for societal existence—and providing freedom from fear remains the most basic duty of government.

There are two main areas in which a democratic government must preserve the peace to be effective. It must protect the citizenry from foreign attacks, fears from without, and it must protect the citizenry from crime and dictatorship, fears from within.

1. Fears From Without

Thanks to the consistent efforts of every American President since Woodrow Wilson, we now have very little to fear from aggression from foreign powers that could threaten our national existence by direct conquest. The continuing challenge before the Presidents and Congresses that will lead us through the twenty-first century will be to strike a balance on United States involvement in areas of the world where war or instability will compromise our vital interests. We have no legitimate responsibilities toward other nations that are inconsistent with our duties to ourselves.

Vital National Interests

However, if we define our vital interests as matters with an immediate impact on the integrity of our borders, as some would have us do, we could withdraw within a shell, like a turtle, and pretend to let the world go by. If we did so, we eventually would stick our corporate head back out to find the same world, except it would be more unstable than when we withdrew, and that instability would be creeping ever nearer our borders because of our lack of vision.

We do have a vital national interest in the establishment of democracy in other nations. We do have a vital national interest in the integrity of the borders of democratic nations. Democracies are less likely to engage in wars with their neighbors. Those with free presses allow their people to be adequately informed, and adequately informed people are less likely to wage war for foolish reasons. If chances for war are lessened, our chances of being pulled into an expanded conflict in the future are lessened.

The introduction of American troops into an area should always be done with great deliberation, or according to a set plan or policy established and continued with great deliberation and general consensus. We should always keep communication channels open and be ready to mediate disputes when our participation is invited. And we should seek invitations to mediate to avoid being required to militate.

We must also prioritize, lending greater emphasis and attention where it is most due. Helping democracy take root in Russia was our top foreign policy imperative before the 9/11/01 Tragedies. The Soviet Union never attacked us on our soil, but Middle Eastern terrorists now have to devastating effect. It is disappointing that in 2004 we still do not have a fully stable and democratic Russia robustly cooperating to maintain international peace. We need their cooperation to keep our own burdens tolerable and to help them reduce theirs in the future. Furthermore, to the extent that all nations, especially Russia, join together in trade participation, war-causing nationalistic pressures will be lessened. We and the other United Nations must help democracy and market economies take hold in Russia by using every reasonable means at our disposal.

We must also keep foremost in our minds the fact that much of the nuclear bomb material that could potentially be secured by terrorists remains within the borders of the former Soviet Union. Thus, a focus on enhancing the stability of Russia and its former Soviet neighbors must be a part of our focus on eradicating international terrorism in the interest of our national security.

We must prevent the spread of nuclear weapons. No other force under the control of mankind has the ability to so suddenly cause massive destruction. Once again, expansion of trading opportunities, particularly with those countries that already have nuclear weapons and those which have shown a desire to obtain such weapons, will lead to greater participation and cooperation in eliminating this threat. As trade participation expands, true worldwide embargoes against aggressor nations and nations that support terrorism will be more likely to convince offenders to change their ways without force, which we should always try to do as a first resort.

The First Question

We can take a lesson on military participation by the United States in any conflict, whether or not UN action is involved, from the French assistance to our revolution. Our French allies were willing to commit logistical support, primarily through their navy, after we were willing to risk our own lives in the conflict.

A threshold premise of our foreign policy should be that American lives will never be put at military risk on foreign soil when the natural defenders and maintainers of that soil, the citizens of the foreign nation, are unwilling to risk their own lives in the battle against their oppressors. That threshold being met, training, financial and logistical support are the only reasonable options absent a threat to the direct interests of the United States so strong that it can maintain political support despite the harsh images of war that will inevitably follow the introduction of American troops. We saw support for humanitarian action in Somalia quickly undermined when pictures emerged of our dead soldiers' bodies being desecrated. With humanitarian goals playing an ever-larger part in the current Iraqi action, we are beginning to see similar erosion following the horrendous images that have emerged from there. Failure in Iraq is not an acceptable alternative. We should all be relieved to be seeing an endgame slowly beginning to materialize there.

Some chide those who have wanted to see an endgame more quickly implemented in Iraq with being willing to cut and run, often using Vietnam and Somalia as examples where they apparently believe we should not have disengaged. However, if we find ourselves involved in a conflict where we should not have been in the first place, like Vietnam or Somalia, the sooner we cut our losses and extract our forces after the situation turns against us, the better. We have more than fifty thousand families that have been grievously harmed because we did not acknowledge the error of Vietnam sooner. An error cannot be corrected by duration.

We have had a recurring problem deciding where to draw the line of involvement once troops have been introduced. In Korea, we participated as a part of the UN to repulse the invading North. But, by carrying the battle deeply into the territory of the invader, the bordering Chinese army seized an excuse to intervene. The entry of the Chinese into the hostilities prolonged the conflict for years.

In Vietnam, also a nation bordering China, we acted without the UN. Even so, the memory of Korea combined with other factors, primarily a concern over a potential nuclear confrontation with the Soviet Union, to keep us from substantially crossing the border into North Vietnam. This prolonged the conflict and increased our loss of life at the same time that it insured our eventual retreat.

In Iraq in 1991, American troops were part of a virtually unhindered UN advance that stopped shortly after crossing the border of the aggressor nation. We did so in compliance with the UN objectives that had been spelled out before the operation began. These limiting objectives were agreed upon even though the only credible threat to us near the borders of the Iraqi aggressor, the Russians, had agreed with our part in the operation. The decision to halt the advance left a meddling terrorist regime in power and required the maintenance of military no-fly zones in the north and south of Iraq for more than a decade.

We can learn from all of these examples. Where there is no credible threat to us on or near the borders of an aggressor nation, we should always demand total victory. Anything short of that objective does not give our people an adequate return on the blood and treasure invested. It is this very factor that explains why the 2003 Iraqi invasion has retained substantial public support in spite of numerous missteps. We wanted the job finished in 1991.

We are not citizens of an impoverished nation who long for the slim wages of mercenaries. Americans are accustomed to satisfaction, and there is no area in which we may more justifiably demand to be satisfied than in military endeavors by which we lose some of our best people to death, injury and illness. Our satisfaction at only losing a few score brave young people killed in the 1991 Iraqi action have long since faded away as thousands of our soldiers have languished with mysterious medical problems owning service in the Persian Gulf as the only common denominator.

We should decline any future invitations for or inclinations toward the participation of United States troops in any UN action in which total victory is not the objective when there is no legitimate military threat on or near the borders of the focus nation. In the case of 1991 Iraq, we should have been able to advance to the death, capture or banishment of Hussein after establishing a defensive perimeter to the east to prevent meddling from Iran. This perimeter would have needed to be maintained only until a new Iraqi government could have gained credible control of the nation.

Had the Kurds broken away from Iraq in the north, it would have only been the just result of the military and environmental terrorism launched by Saddam Hussein. Turkey, an ally of ours which has a significant Kurdish population, has proven well capable of maintaining its borders and could have easily continued to do so against a potentially antagonistic, but small, Kurdish border state.

A new Iraq could have quickly been accepted back into the family of nations following the 1991 action, had that action been taken to its natural fruition. The essential territorial and economic integrity of Iraq would have been maintained and a source of persistent irritation would have been eliminated from the world 12 tears earlier.

Had we met with today's insurgency in 1991, we would have had a much larger and more internationally diverse and financed UN force there on the ground to deal with it than we have now. Of course, we have now traded maintenance of no-fly zones for full occupation of the Iraqi nation and the capture of Hussein, with rapidly escalating costs in the matter, both in blood and money.

Whatever mistakes we may have made with regard to Iraq, it will always be Saddam Hussein's fault that the country was occupied. Had he not reveled in games of chicken and taunting, he would still be in power and his country would have probably been out from under sanctions years ago. There is no credible doubt that Saddam Hussein repeatedly defied the UN mandates and agreements that he made to bring the 1991 conflict to a close.

Much has been made of whether we should leave immediately or stay on indefinitely until Iraq is secured, having our people die and our money spent along the way. But, there are almost always more than 2 choices in such matters. It is encouraging that we now appear to be binding ourselves to other alternatives that may be more constructive. Hopefully, the situation will progress to the point that we can observe the long overdue trial of Saddam Hussein for crimes against humanity with satisfaction instead of buyer's remorse.

In Korea and Vietnam, after notifying potentially threatening border powers and allies of the aggressors (China and the Soviet Union in these cases) of our harmless intentions towards them, we could have advanced to the point of taking a significant area of the aggressors' territories and stopped to establish strong defensive lines. From that point, we could have negotiated with the aggressors for a return of their territories in exchange for peace. Had we followed this policy in Korea, the initial predictions of only a brief conflict could have possibly been realized instead of the prolonged war that resulted.

When the risks of following either a total victory or a conquer-and-trade-back policy are too great, as they may well have been in Vietnam, then we have no business placing our troops in the conflict. We are legitimately limited to providing supplies, training and information. We have no reasonably affordable likelihood of either victory or credible withdrawal in such cases. The North Vietnamese knew this and simply waited for the inevitable call home.

We should also mentally place ourselves in the places of the border powers and allies of our enemies and realize that we would surely attack if an invading nation approached our borders through a neighboring nation. We would also seek to save face in the event of an attack on one of our allies, even if the attack had been provoked by a foolish mistake on the part of our ally.

Following these methodical approaches in these conflicts could have resulted in more successful conclusions. However, the key premise is that we should never introduce troops to a situation where we cannot obtain returns sufficient to justify taking the risks of making military gains by which we can achieve undeniable victory, or at least negotiate credible peaceful withdrawal.

As with securing freedom from want, altruism is not a valid motivation for international military action. We are corporately entitled to receive tangible benefits from the actions of our government. This entitlement is absolutely the strongest when the government action concerns participation in foreign wars.

The United Nations

We should continue to support and encourage positive United Nations involvement in international disputes. The greatest military conflict yet known to mankind, World War II, was a true example of the world's nations uniting to defeat common foes bent on brutal conquest. The long-term UN mission of preventing future world conflagrations should never be forgotten in the midst of the organization's mistakes in implementing means to achieve that mission.

The 1991 UN action in Iraq, which prevented a significant percentage of global oil reserves from falling under despotic control, was vital to the economic health of the world, once Iraq had invaded Kuwait. However, the heady predictions of a new world order after this UN success have quickly been crushed by the heavy weight of practical reality. We have since very painfully learned that a policy of squelching all conflict is unworkable.

The citizens of the great democracies, who must inevitably shoulder the burdens in finance and lives for any successful large-scale UN action, are quite naturally unwilling to do so unless they perceive some significant return to themselves for sake of the risks. Televised images of the carnage of foreign wars and oppression suffered by others, and the sympathy that understandably results, cannot sustain our people's motivation for war beyond the point at which the acts of brutality begin to be exercised against our own kith and kin. This was the lesson of Somalia in 1992 and 1993. We did well not to relearn it in Haiti in 1994.

The Balkan conflict of the 1990s has since passed well into the background, with occasional news of the World Court proceedings with Milosevic the only reminder for most of us. Like many Americans, I had great misgivings while that conflict was building toward possible introduction of significant numbers of American troops into harm's way. And, also like many Americans, I took a somewhat cavalier attitude about the suffering that people were enduring there, until I met the face of that suffering in my own living room in the form of several young brothers and sisters that came here as refugees.

These young people (ranging in age from about 4 to 18) and their extended family faced horrors that most of us have only heard and read about. And I could not look into the intelligent eyes of the oldest brother without knowing that he could have easily taken a place in a mass grave.

The extent to which I can maintain a cold heart toward those that endured the same type of horrors in Iraq only reflects the fact they I have not similarly looked them in the eyes. Yet, the feelings of the heart must be bounded by the knowledge of the head. We must accept the fact that troops with peacekeeping or humanitarian missions that are placed into the middle of a war zone are inevitably caught in the crossfire of local military and political struggles. Sometimes war zones have to be acknowledged as acceptable zones of conflict wherein the residents fight out their own convictions to conclusion. Nations bordering such zones should be provided an opportunity to have peacekeepers stationed along their borders, directed toward the conflict and with authority to attack with full force if the warring parties carry the battle outside of the acceptable zone.

Israel

Israel had its introduction to suicide terrorists with shadowy connections to organized governments long before we did. Until such terrorists are marginalized by the civilized world, they will continue to be lionized by the majority of the populations in the Middle East, and will be thus encouraged to continue their profoundly wasteful, destructive and murderous acts. It is hard to imagine them marginalized without Israel yielding to the internationally recognized 1967 borders.

The terrorists operating in Israel appear to be strategically engaged in a war of attrition in which their primary method of keeping support in the masses has been by pointing to retaliatory strikes that sometimes consume the innocent along with the criminals. Why else would they have reserved some of their most heinous acts, bus bombings and the like, for just before Israeli elections? Surely they anticipated that such acts would tend to move the voters toward the candidates most likely to retaliate most harshly.

The same type of strategic thinking was implemented to the opposite effect in 2004 in Spain. Train bombings, apparently by Islamic militants, were factors in the election of a Socialist government that had promised to act quickly to withdraw Spain's small contingent of forces from Iraq. The obvious terrorist intention in Spain was to peel off an ally from the U.S.-led coalition

Many well-intended Americans may be fueling Middle Eastern conflict by adhering to a Biblical description of an ancient land grant without considering the modern context. One may or may not believe that ancient Israel was established at the behest of the Eternal. However, honesty requires admitting that the modern State of Israel was established under UN authority in the 1940s, largely in response to the profound suffering of the Jewish people under Hitler. I suppose that considering the UN as a proxy for the Almighty would constitute idolatry under all legitimate theologies.

The answer may return that the Bible also teaches that the Almighty uses flawed human governments and institutions as tools in His omnipotent hands. No doubt. But in the Biblical example of King Cyrus being so used, as recorded in Ezra, did the returned Israeli exiles take it upon themselves to exceed the boundaries set by the human authority? Hardly. They acted cooperatively and thereby received its protection. Ezekiel even describes the same relationship relative to Israel and its Babylonian conquerors in chapter 17.

It is also a historical fact that the integrity of Israel's internationally recognized borders was compromised more than once by attacks from neighboring countries, which precipitated their retaliation and taking of the bordering lands, most of which we now know as the West Bank. It is hard to blame them for now seeking to build a solid defense wall after rogue acts of nations and individuals have caused them so much pain so many times. However, it is also hard to envision any outcome other than continuing violence so long as that wall, or any other boundary structure, is built other than along the recognized international boundary.

International Terrorism

While no foreign government currently threatens our national existence, there are some that support international terrorism that can cause us tremendous damage.

When financial or organizational ties to a foreign government can be established relative to a terrorist act against our people or our substantial interests, we should consider it an act of war and respond accordingly. The connection was clear with the Taliban Afghan government that harbored Bin Laden after the 9/11 Trage-dies, and our military action to destroy it was therefore entirely justified. But we must be wise and focused during these perilous times to preserve the lives of our people, our international stature and our money.

A TV channel out of Charlotte, North Carolina, used to broadcast a favorite show for my adolescent friends and me: bullfights. A bullfight is a cruel spectacle that I would not care to watch now, but it may have an important message for us after the 9/11 Tragedies. The magnificent beast, powerful and proud, is first gouged and lanced by the picadors until its back flows with blood. Then, when it is filled with pain and rage, yet still at full strength, in walks the skinny matador in his ridiculous outfit. Who knows what is in the animal's mind as it repeatedly passes mere inches from what should be its true target, to charge through the extended red cape? I suspect that it thinks it is delivering mortal blows by goring another bull in its vulnerable side. But, it is wasting its energy. On rare occasions the bull will not be fooled and gores the matador, tossing him into the air like a pitiful rag-doll before trampling him, with the formerly distracting cape flutter-ing powerlessly to the ground.

But usually the once proud bull ends up standing exhausted in the midst of the ring, drained of breath and blood, with not a single charge left in its power. At that point, the Matador taunts its weakness, standing barely a foot in front of its panting face and harmless horns for just a moment, before striking the death blow by driving a sword into the back of its neck. We must be smarter than the easily distracted bull.

Saddam Hussein's Iraq was certainly more than the equivalent of the mata-dor's red cape. For instance, it has been widely reported that the families of sui-cide bombers attacking Israel were being awarded with bounties out of Iraq. Yet, we cannot allow even Iraq to distract from the hunt for Bin Laden. We have learned, sometimes by Bin Laden's own voice and videos, that he had a hand in the first attempt to topple the Twin Towers, and in the bombings of our naval ship, our military barracks, our East African embassies and, most tragically, in the toppling of our Twin Towers and bombing of our Pentagon on 9/11/01. He and his followers murdered almost 3000 of our people on that one awful day, not to mention the scores of lives snuffed out in other attacks. We must do several very difficult things at once, in Afghanistan, in Iraq and in the international terrorist hunt, and that is why it is so costly.

The harsh truth of warfare, whether it is waged on a grand scale or by isolated acts of violence, is that fire must be fought with fire, and force met with stronger force. We have the capacity to unleash unequaled force, and we should be willing to do so when necessary, whether or not we are participating with the UN.

We need to maintain that capacity, both to meet foreign aggression when necessary and to enjoy the economic benefits of a strong military. If we allow ourselves to lose the capacity to strike swiftly and severely, we can surely expect an increase in aggressive actions against our people and international interests. Protecting this capability will enhance our freedoms from fear of international war and terrorists, as well as domestic terrorism.

2. Violent Fear From Within

We see it almost every day on television and in the papers. We hear it on the radios. It is news of violent crime: a young girl gunned down over twenty dollars at an automatic bank teller machine; a child shot while sleeping in his bed; an old woman raped; an old man bludgeoned; thousands of acres and scores of homes burned by an arsonist; a man set on fire by strangers; a harmless pet cruelly attacked; a veteran killed at home after surviving dangers abroad; a random driver shot by a sniper; children lured to be tortured and murdered. We have stopped imagining that we have seen the worst, because some evil person is always ready to commit a worse crime than the ones before.

And we hardly even consider the countless robberies, shopliftings, burglaries, carjackings, kidnappings, stalkings, intimidations and harassments. After all, we rationalize, it could have been worse, physical integrity or life could have just as easily been lost.

And we set about to defend ourselves: by adding our new guns to the more than 200 million already in circulation in our nation; by adding locks and bolts and alarms and bars to our doors and windows; by staying at home; by refusing to know our neighbors. Yet, we feel the nagging uneasiness of a lack of power to truly protect ourselves from the violence that strikes innocent people every day.

One thing is certain. No matter how free we are to speak or worship, and even if everyone gets a good job and the government is brought out of debt and taxes are eliminated, and even if all foreign nations become our friends and partners in improving the conditions of the world's people, it will all be empty if we live in fear that we or those we love will be hurt by aggressive, malicious, disrespectful, manipulative people. Fear is not an American value.

But another fact that we should recognize, and that can give the honest citizenry hope, is illustrated by another Old Testament story. The prophet and his assistant were in a town surrounded by the enemy. The assistant, understandably terrified, asked what could be done. The prophet calmly prayed that the assistant's eyes be opened to see the truth. After the prayer, the assistant looked again and saw that an angelic army was there to defend them. They had been there all along, but they were unseen.

Like the assistant, we should know that there is a many times greater army of decent hardworking citizens than is on the side of evil in this land. We are largely unseen, and we only need leadership and organization to quickly rid the cities and countryside of the elements of intimidation that have hindered the peace of our lives.

Consider a new day, when an old man and woman can confidently take a private evening walk hand in hand through the city streets, when a young woman and her baby can peacefully drive wherever she chooses to go, when no threat of violence lurks at the highway rest stop to prevent an inexpensive nap during night driving, when retail workers are not threatened by shoplifters or robbers. This can be America. In fact, this must be America if we are to progress to a mature democracy. For until the crime problem is solved, and its monstrous wastes eliminated, we cannot fully concentrate on putting our energies into solving the emerging problems of the twenty-first century. International terrorism, Iraq, Russia and China all vie for preeminence in foreign policy. However, the duties of domestic government dictate that crime control must be a preeminent focus.

The Criminal Justice System

Mercy is the province of God, not government. Government only has justification for following a policy of active benevolence when that policy benefits the population in furthering domestic prosperity and peace.

Thus, merciful and generous (liberal, if you will) programs in areas such as educational grants and loans and job placement and training can help citizens be more productive and pay more taxes, lowering the general tax rate while increasing the general level of satisfaction among the citizenry. Programs such as food stamps and public housing provide the basic necessities of life, discouraging criminality out of need.

However, the incentives to maintain any mercy basis in the criminal law system are minimal. For every criminal effectively rehabilitated by the system to become a contributing taxpayer, several return to their old ways of intimidation and banditry upon release, often after serving only a fraction of the time sentenced.

The arguments in favor of the penal system as it currently operates, including a juvenile justice system that allows predatory youths to evade responsibility for their acts, are consistent with selective tenets of the Christian religion: mercy; forgiveness; rehabilitation; and reconciliation. Jesus Christ said to not even resist evil, to turn the other cheek if assaulted and to give more than demanded if sued.

Selective introduction of such distinctly religious aims into the government business of crime control violates the spirit of the constitutional separation of church and state. While individual persons of whatever religion may, as a matter of personal conscience, choose to deal passively with aggression, no group of religious adherents has a right to impose the responsibility of distinctly religious behavior upon fellow citizens.

Our laws against offenses such as murder and thievery, while shared with most religions, need no religious justification. They promote general peace and prosperity. However, institutionalized coercion of societal forgiveness for violent acts can satisfy no corporate goals other than those of the heart, where the government has no place.

When religious conscience dictates passivity in the face of aggression, the religious inclination should be exercised in confidence that a government represented by the statue of blind justice will discourage aggression and punish it if it occurs. The aggressive predatory criminal is not only the enemy of the immediate victim; he is the enemy of democracy. And lovers of freedom have a duty to prevent him from harming another person. For the sake of society, for the other innocents who may be injured by the same villain who may have dared to injure us, we have a responsibility to see that punishment for crimes is sure and swift. Punishment of the wicked and praise of the just are foundational behaviors by which we learn our object lessons from early ages. When the system of just rewards breaks down, frustration enters on the part of the just and boldness appears on the part of the wicked.

Constitutional guarantees that we regret on behalf of others today may be those that we cherish for ourselves tomorrow. The problem is not the rights of the accused or even the number of the accused. The problem is the number of offenses that some of the accused are allowed to commit. We should provide enough government funds to build humane prison space to house criminals for full sentence lengths, including life sentences without possibility of parole for the most violent offenders. Taking the short-sighted approach of crowding two or more prisoners into an area designed for one will require the courts to intervene and demand that all humans be treated with at least minimal decency, with shortened sentences required to relieve overcrowding.

We should also acknowledge the cathartic effect provided to the families and friends of a victim when a murderer is executed, or the peace of mind that can be provided to rape victims by ensuring long-term incarceration for the perpetrators. It is arrogant for the uninjured to lecture victims of violent crime about the degree of satisfaction that should suffice. Enough police should be available, and visible, to discourage bad actors. The tax laws can also be used to encourage hiring private security officers for stores and parking lots.

Back to the Honest Living Wage

Adding prison space and additional officers to the social framework can preserve a sense of security. However, their effect could be like placing a heavy lid on a pot of boiling water. The surface may look stable, but the pressure will build underneath and may eventually be vented, either in spurts or an explosion. So, there must also be positive social responses to crime that are not authoritarian.

The network of business volunteers that accepts and trains ex-convicts for work after prison release should be greatly expanded. This activity can also be encouraged by the tax code.

As with welfare reform, any meaningful progress in reforming criminal behavior in the non-predatory must include establishment of an honest living wage. Unskilled ex-convicts cannot reasonably be expected to follow the path of productivity upon prison release if they are freed to jobs by which they cannot support themselves and their families. The honest living wage is also necessary to prevent the unfortunate potential cycle of arrest, imprisonment and release to a business willing to place an ex-convict in a good job becoming a way out of poverty. All adult American citizens should be able to earn an honest living wage for their work.

Yet, we should not be deceived into thinking that more good jobs will erase crime. An honest living wage will only take away excuses for thievery; it will not rid us of thieves. This is well proven by economic predators who, without financial needs, engage in ruthless business practices, apparently as a form of sport. Their moral counterparts, violent criminal predators, are not driven by life's necessities to harm the innocent. They are driven by lusts for power and control over others. The fact that they can also make a living by their antisocial behavior is a bonus to them.

It can be easier to get money by crime than work. A thief can steal a piece of jewelry in seconds, sell it within the hour and have more money before lunch on Monday than he could have gained by honest work in a month. Economic predation at least takes the discipline to understand how businesses and markets work. But any idiot with a gun or knife can be a violent predator.

A corollary to job placement and establishment of an honest living wage should dictate that prison work be required, and that the money earned, at a sub-living wage, be substantially funneled to a victim compensation fund for recovery of uninsured financial losses from crime. Criminals living by predation because the money is easier by crime than by disciplined job performance should be put on notice that the punishment upon conviction will be harder work than that which is being avoided. The only good behavior by which a property criminal should be able to gain early release should be by full restitution.

Restitution for property crimes should continue after the appointed prison sentence has been served. An honest person may toil for years to financially recover from a bad business choice. A criminal should be subject to at least the same consequences for dishonest and predatory actions.

The option for early release upon restitution for costs such as medical expenses should not apply to rapists and violent attackers since these crimes are not reducible to financial cost. They are crimes against life and freedom. Perpetrators of such offenses should serve the time sentenced without parole possibilities.

Bearing Arms Rightly

A discussion of violence in America is incomplete without a discussion of arms. The Second Amendment to our Constitution guarantees a right to bear arms. Some have argued that the language of the amendment provides only for the right within the context of military service, as the "well regulated militia" language suggests, and they seem to feel to be granting a great exemption when they allow that hunters should have their weapons.

However, this is not an honest reading of the Amendment or history. No person of the 1700s, when the Amendment was written, would have dreamed of restricting use of a weapon by which the people could gain their food or defend themselves. The Second Amendment is about survival and self-defense, against aggressors foreign or domestic.

The concept of honest historical context also enters into the equation from the other side of the ledger. For instance, even those who purport to argue for an absolute right to bear arms cannot seriously suggest (or will never be taken seriously if they do suggest) that an individual has a right to have a personal nuclear bomb. There is no doubt that these instruments are arms. We pushed our nation to the financial precipice in an arms race with the Soviet Union over just such weapons. And a cornerstone of our foreign policy under every President since World War II has been slowing the spread of nuclear weapons technology, international gun control.

While we should have high admiration for our nation's founders, we should not worship them as gods who saw the future and incorporated it into the Constitution. The fact that they provided for the continuation of slavery and the counting of individual slaves as three-fifths of a person shows that they were quite imperfect beings, doing their best within the context of their time to provide as stable and efficient a government as they could. The Constitution had to be amended ten times before it was acceptable to the country, and it has been amended more than a dozen other times since. It is not Holy Writ.

The point here is that men in the 1780's, when a trained marksman may have been able to load and fire three inaccurate rounds from a rifle in the space of a minute, had no comprehension of individual weapons that could level cities, or that could clear a street of dozens of people in a matter of seconds. They prepared a Constitution that could be shaped for the future, not one that incorporated the future.

Once one accepts the obvious fact that some weapons are too dangerous for individual ownership or wide dissemination, we can look at the Second Amendment and guns in a more balanced manner. In short, there is no valid cause for a private citizen to own a weapon more powerful than to fire a few rounds in not-so-rapid succession in case of a need for self-defense or hunting.

Those who wish to maintain broad availability of high-powered firearms are likely to have ulterior motives unrelated to reasonable use. They may wish to profit from the sale of the weapons. Or, they may wish to establish the capability for armed rebellion or to maintain superiority over competitors for other illegal activities, such as related to drug trafficking.

Efforts toward armed overthrow of the government are referred to as illegal activity akin to drug trafficking for the obvious reason that the Second Amendment to the United States Constitution refers to possession of arms within the context of government under that Constitution. The same document also makes specific reference in Article III, Section 3 to the crime of treason.

The people who imagine and plot such things as overthrowing our government are disgruntled misfits who have been unable to get their extremist positions adopted through the legitimate means of the ballot. So, they hope to be able to resort to the bullet or the bomb. They would fully deserve the annihilation that they would receive for embarking upon such treason.

Even so, our people should spare them the tragedy in the interest of promoting domestic tranquility. They should have the opportunity for ownership of inappropriate weapons removed, just as should be done for all other parts of criminal culture.

Limiting access to such weapons should also be seen as favoring business. It has become too familiar to hear of an angry person, justifiably fired from a job, who returns to the property of his former employer to rain havoc with an assault weapon. Terminating an employee from a job is stressful enough without the supervisor or employer having to be concerned about a maniac returning to commit murder and mayhem. While it is true that the maniac could also retaliate with a non-automatic rifle, shotgun, pistol, or even a knife, the potential for damage would be markedly limited if there was no ready access to weapons of volume human extermination.

We should also acknowledge that we have a warrior heritage. This plays out in our aggressive entertainments and sports. And we are heavily armed, with more than 200 million appropriate firearms in circulation. We need to have an organized outlet by which lawful gun owners may responsibly exercise their constitutional right to bear arms within the context of the document.

We already have a full-time military, reserve forces and state National Guard forces. Some states also have non-military volunteer militias that aid the National Guard in the event of natural disasters or other acute hardships.

Our heavily armed status and the existence of unregulated paramilitary militias that thrive on combinations of racism and paranoia point to the need for expanding legitimate state militias into an organized fourth force. Such a system will allow willing men and women to meet periodically for drills and training under the supervision of trained and authorized military personnel, satisfying the requirement of the Second Amendment that such groups be "well regulated." Groups could be organized by cities, towns and counties, and could engage in healthy competition in marksmanship and strength.

Such a system would channel the natural aggression of young men into positive expressions. It would foster responsibility, citizenship and sportsmanship. It would provide a trained organization of far greater numbers than we currently have for disaster relief. It would further marginalize the criminal weapons element, and it would serve notice to that element that the honest citizenry is armed and trained to protect itself. And, in the event that any foreign nation does ever dare to attempt to invade our borders, it will ensure that it receives swift destruction. These results are exactly those that the Second Amendment, one of the foundational cornerstones of our government, was designed to bring about.

3. Political Fear From Within

This final fear is so remote that it hardly enters the mind of an American citizen. It is the fear of dictatorship. It has been made remote by our system of government that has allowed the arming of the private citizenry, and has fostered free flow of information and balance of opinions.

The Electoral College

Our fortunate history has been that even when an especially liberal or conservative or militaristic or charismatic President has managed to get elected, none has approached establishing a degree of power that legitimately threatened democracy. There has always been an opposition force to moderate when a President may have wished to impose extremes.

While we may not experience the fear of dictatorship, we should still seek to understand why we have not had this curse imposed upon us, so that we can protect against inadvertently or intentionally dismantling the source of our stable and moderate government during a moment in time when emotion may overrun good sense. The primary source of our stable government has been the Electoral College.

Our Constitution does not allow for direct voting for the President and Vice-President. The votes that we cast in our individual states go towards the selection of electors that equal the total members that the state has in the United States House of Representatives and Senate.

Most states require all of their electors to vote for the Presidential and Vice Presidential candidates that gain the most votes in the individual state. This holds true whether the race is decided in the state by one vote or one million votes. After the public votes, the electors meet to actually elect the President and Vice-President, based upon the state-by-state results.

Thus, in the 1992 election, Clinton was elected by a large Electoral College majority although his actual votes only exceeded those of Bush by about five percent of the total of more than 100 million cast, about forty-three percent to about thirty-eight percent. And Ross Perot, who received about nineteen percent of the total votes cast, received zero electoral votes since he did not have the leading vote total in any state. Similar results occurred in 1968 in the Nixon, Humphrey and Wallace race.

Even more skewed results occasionally occur. In the election of 1824, the candidate receiving the most votes, Andrew Jackson (forty-two percent), lost the presidency to John Quincy Adams (thirty-two percent). Neither of the four candidates running (also including William Crawford and Henry Clay, each with thirteen percent) was able to gain the necessary electoral votes, but Adams was able to muster a majority of votes by state delegations in the House, the fallback option under the Constitution. And, of course, we have since had the 2000 election. Gore exceeded George W. Bush's popular vote total by about 500,000 but was denied the Presidency when the disputed Florida electors went to Bush.

Cries went up from Gore supporters in 2000, Perot supporters in 1992 and, no doubt, Jackson supporters in 1824 that the Electoral College system is undemocratic. In a sense, it is: but we need to consider (1) what the results of using it have been; and (2) what the alternatives to using it would be.

The Electoral College protects the rights of citizens of small states by requiring that a candidate for President of the United States must receive strong support in many states to be elected. A person needs a majority of electoral votes to take office. When an Electoral College majority does not result, the decision goes to the House of Representatives for a vote of state delegations, where a majority is again required, as occurred in 1824.

The requirement of Electoral College majorities has led to the two-party system that has dominated American politics since the early 1800's. The two-party system is sometimes attacked as a basis of corruption and stalemate. However, it has required that mainstream thinking dominate in both parties. When either major party has gotten too liberal or conservative for the general public, it has been awarded with presidential election defeats until stands were moderated, allowing a return to competitive elections.

We see this pattern clearly throughout the last century. After the Republicans holding sway in the 1920s and 1930s (Harding, Coolidge, and Hoover) refused to respond to the needs of the people in a changing economy, the Democrats gained five straight election victories under Roosevelt and Truman.

Brief ebbs and flows of general balance held sway from 1952 through 1980, with a Republican (Eisenhower) followed by two Democrats (Kennedy and Johnson), followed by Republicans (Nixon and Ford who, of course, completed Nixon's second term without election), who were followed by a Democrat (Carter). The Republicans once again earned the presidency through two Reagan terms and one of Bush, who was followed by another Democrat, Clinton, and another Republican, George W. Bush. Thus, the nation keeps itself aright through the decades by shifting between the political spectrums.

The clear result of the Electoral College and the two-party system is that any successful President must focus upon moderation and negotiation. Thus, our government remains relatively stable, even when a conservative President replaces a moderate or liberal one, or vice versa. Combine this factor with an appointed and life-tenured Supreme Court and a popularly elected Congress and dictatorship becomes virtually impossible. This is part of the genius of government under our Constitution.

Some people argue that our system makes governing too difficult. However, they should stop and think of the alternatives.

Some misguided people have said that a benevolent dictatorship would be a better government. They reason that a wise and kind person, unrestricted by elections and negotiations, could better govern our affairs, while sparing us the trouble of voting, deciding and, generally, thinking. Such a government would merely be a monarchy. Even in the rare cases when a good monarch has reigned, who was there to follow except a typically incompetent spouse, son or daughter, or perhaps a sibling or cousin clever and ruthless enough to take over?

We should also consider the parliamentary form of democracy. This is Britain's form of government, serving under the figurehead monarchy.

In parliamentary democracies, the people vote for representatives and the group or party of representatives that gets the most members elected in the legislative body chooses the nation's Prime Minister. Unless the party with the most officials elected gets more than fifty percent of the available offices, which is not often the case since these governments inevitably fragment into three or more parties, the leader of the party with the most members elected must form a coalition government by negotiating with one or more of the other parties.

Consequently, extremist parties with only a few elected members and minimal public support can hold exaggerated influence because they are needed to form the governing majority. These fringe groups can politically hold nations hostage by threatening to withdraw their support.

Compare this unfortunate situation with our Electoral College dominated government. The President of the United States is almost always constrained to reach out to moderates of the opposition party to form a governing majority, an act that often requires him to step away from extremists in his own party. Thus, our government is only held under the sway of majority opinion, the exact result that democracy is supposed to yield.

The parliamentary system often leads to unstable governments led by people who are rarely supported by a majority of the citizenry. Consider the 1993 Canadian election. There were five major parties in the running. The way the votes broke down, the Liberal party won a landslide majority of seats in the parliament, allowing selection of the recently retired Cretien as Prime Minister, by receiving less than forty-three percent of the national vote. The vote breakdown also resulted in decimation of the Progressive Conservative party, which won only three seats in Parliament, despite the facts that (1) it received the second highest total number of votes throughout the country, and (2) it had been the governing party for almost the entire preceding decade.

Consider those results against the forty-three percent of votes received in America by President Clinton in 1992, and the legitimate claims that he lacked overwhelming support for his program. The difference between the Clinton government that, with forty-three percent, eschewed bipartisanship to its peril, and the Cretien government which, with less than forty-three percent, was able to rule much more forcefully, is the Electoral College.

Think of how pitiful and splintered our government would be if it was under a parliamentary system or a system of direct election of the President and Vice-President: if there were no Electoral College to essentially force competing ideas to find a home in one of two major parties. Though we would probably continue to have two or, at most, three main parties, they would be much weaker. They would be joined by several, maybe dozens, of fringe parties focused upon race, religion, age, area, vocation and every other point of division in society.

This type of splintered government has resulted in about 50 separate governments in Italy since 1948. The number has to be estimated because they come and go so quickly. This type also allows for fluke results, such as the previously mentioned example of the decimation of the Progressive Conservative party in Canada. Or, elimination of the Electoral College could lead to an essentially one party government, such as has traditionally prevailed in Mexico. Multi-party government leads to confusion that makes our legislative gridlock look like the workings of a well-oiled machine, and one party government tends toward unfettered corruption.

Our Electoral College protects us from such terrible results. It has provided stability and two strong parties in which most reasonable persons can find enough agreement to identify and participate. It is a key part of the primary stroke of genius of our founders: an extension to the presidency of the same principles that had allowed adoption of the Constitution, the Great Compromise of two houses of Congress, one based on population, The House of Representatives, and one with equal representation for each state, The Senate. This ingenious mechanism prevents the more populous states from totally dominating American politics.

Citizens opposed to the Electoral College in Tennessee, Utah, Wyoming and most of the other states should ask themselves whether they really want to be governed entirely out of New York, Texas and California. The Electoral College has promoted peace and a sense of equality among us, and it will continue to do so for centuries after the ill-informed arguments of its detractors are forgotten.

Affirmative Action

By way of analogy, we should also consider the persistent national tension over the issue of affirmative action, the government-encouraged advancement of particular groups within society. The fact of the matter is that this issue may be one of history's greatest non-issues.

It has been through the courts that programs for the advancement of women and racial minorities have been enforced and justified. It is also through the courts that such programs are now being modified on behalf of other citizens who have had opportunities unjustifiably limited. If we are patient, we will find that balance will result through our elective and judicial processes, just like the system was designed to provide.

However, the promise of long-term balance is hardly soothing to a person who is suffering today by way of perceived injustice. But before giving way to frustration and generally condemning a system that has certainly provided opportunity to millions who never had it before and might not have had it otherwise, we should consider whether (1) such a system can be of general benefit, and (2) whether we may not have specifically benefited from a similar system.

The Electoral College, with the many benefits previously described, is simply an affirmative action program for states with small populations, as is the non-population representation provided by the Senate. Whines of despair have not been heard coming from the people of California, New York and Texas because Rhode Island, Wyoming and Alaska each have two Senators and have a definite voice in presidential politics through the Electoral College. The heavily populated states do quite well for themselves despite the help given to the less populated states through our Constitution. In fact, they are much better off by being single parts of the great whole of America than they would be if separated unto themselves.

Furthermore, if some of our citizens who are opposed to affirmative action would broaden their vision, they would understand that they might have even more directly benefited from economic affirmative action. Many people of modest financial backgrounds could have never gone to college without government support by way of grants or low-interest guaranteed loans. Since there are a limited number of spaces for each entering class in our best colleges, it is beyond argument that people who are able to pay their own ways are not accepted for entry every year due to spaces having been allowed to men and women of all races who receive financial aid.

Those able to pay on their own are not denied an education: they simply pay somewhere else. But those not able to pay without assistance gain an education that they could not have otherwise had, and they earn more money and pay more taxes so someone less fortunate than they now are can follow the same path, and so the person who was able to pay his own way through college can pay lower taxes.

The fact that a principle may be generally beneficial does not mean that incorrect application of it may not result in injustice. Thus, ongoing careful review of affirmative action policies is certainly in order.

The question has often been asked of how long such assistance needs to remain in place. After all, the argument goes, black citizens have been able to vote for decades and women for most of a century. The question of "how long" answers itself. If we are still asking it, then time enough has not passed. There will be no more such questions when there is fair access to opportunity. They will fade away like questions over other obsolete laws, such as those concerning horse and buggy operation, when the reasons for the laws have passed.

We are creative enough to develop a generally acceptable solution to any legitimate problems resulting from affirmative action. We just need to apply our energies towards positive decision-making rather than towards divisiveness. We have much more to gain by being together than we do by being apart. For, as with the Electoral College, the spreading of opportunity by reasonable affirmative action has helped create general social peace and stability that have reduced chances for despotism.

A Good Government for a Great People

While dictatorship in America will remain nearly impossible so long as we preserve the Electoral College, we may have a legitimate concern that technology can bring us to a point of effective collective dictatorship under unbridled emotion, a paralyzed system on the fringe of anarchy. Our Congress represents a republican form of government, with elected officials having responsibilities delegated by the people for the performance of the people's business. Mere distance was sufficient to prevent any more direct representation at the time of our nation's founding. Distance is not so limiting today. We can converse across the continent upon a whim. It is even conceivable that the citizenry could use today's technology to directly vote on matters of importance.

We must not allow the convergence of the ability to directly vote and the ability to electronically manipulate public opinion to further undermine our belief in representative government. While our modern cars may provide the ability to travel at very high speeds, we would be unwise to use that ability indiscriminately on the highways. The same is the case as relating to technologies that can allow us to change our stable form of government. Our republican form of government allows for deliberation and reflection over the important issues facing us, rather than a capricious blowing about upon the winds of fickle opinions. It is a wisely conceived government and, contrary to the emotional appeals of some, it is a good government. And the more citizens who participate in it by informed voting for elected officials, the better it will become.

Congressional term limits is an idea that was popular in the late twentieth century. It is ironic that polls showed nearly seventy percent of the population supporting term limits while less than forty percent of those eligible voted in 1994. Congressional turnover or obvious public approval of those elected would eliminate any perceived need for term limits if another thirty percent would bother to vote on a regular basis. Term limits represent merely one more ill conceived idea to program government to do what we should do for ourselves.

We amended the Constitution in 1951 to prevent the election of Presidents to more than two terms, although only one President in history, Franklin Roosevelt, had ever served more than two terms. The fact that others could have served a third term better kept the attention of the Congress, enhancing the possibility that truly strong leadership would be developed in our Chief Executives. The concept of limiting the people's right to elect whomever they choose is based upon at least two negative motivations. It can be based upon the fear of an opponent's success or a pessimistic reservation that our nation has no more giants of democracy to bring forth. There are many more giants of democracy who will yet arise from our midst.

Aside from term limits, the Constitutional limitations on whom can be our President, including that he or she be native born, are sufficient and wise. The native born requirement still makes perfect sense. We should all hope for the success of all of our Presidents. But, there have obviously been some that have just not been very good at the job. This has not made them evil, any more than a poor car mechanic is evil because he wrongly installs a part. But I submit that the last thing that we need, in the way of assuring accountability or avoiding insult, is to have a future President that has been rejected, perhaps in disgrace, retain the option to remove to a trouble-free retirement in his or her foreign native country, especially while we continue to foot the bill for his or her pension, security, office operation and mistakes. The founders believed that our President must have a native connection to this land, and they were wise in that belief.

Our general belief in democracy needs rekindling. Assassinations and Watergate and Vietnam and a hundred different scandals have doused the flame in some hearts, but the embers still glow beneath. Through our veins courses the blood of those who survived slavery and attempts at genocide, of those who carved the greatest nation the world has ever known from a wilderness, of those who humbled the tyrants that would have robbed the world of freedom, of those whose feet bled at Valley Forge.

Ours is the wisest form of government ever developed by man. It has stood the tests of time and trial. It has allowed us to help ourselves, and citizens of the world's far-flung nations. We are extremely ill advised whenever we think of substantively changing it. For the chances are very slim that the changes we make will improve upon the great masterpiece of government under our Constitution.

THE NEXT CENTURY

Our united purpose as citizens of the United States should not be to see how much personal comfort or accumulation that we can amass. Nor should it be so narrow as to only include the benefit of our own kith and kin. It should be nothing short of an unwavering commitment that our present actions will help to build a future in which this nation will stand in better stead 100 years after the dates of our deaths than it does now.

Exercising self-discipline and courage to establish proper balance in the four freedoms during our present generation will secure the financial, cultural and spiritual prosperity available through democracy for today and our tomorrows. It will empower us to live the dreams that those who died before us could only imagine. And it will allow us the privilege and future honor of having secured those and greater dreams for those who will follow us. Arlington's blood and the greatness within us cry out for us to build such a future.

Speech must be free to be an effective tool in the preservation of individual liberties. The people must deny government efforts to control expression that does not reasonably threaten the public good. However, free speech, like all other tools, should be used responsibly. Society has a right to regulate the use of speech and methods of speech delivery when society finances the speech or owns the means of delivery. Society also has a legitimate interest in regulating speech that has been transformed into a weapon against the innocent.

In the age of dazzling technology in which we live, we must be all the more diligent to ensure that the cornerstone of our freedoms, the freedom of speech, shall not be allowed to become the headstone over the grave of democracy. We shall prevent such a possibility from ever occurring by exercising and promoting self-interest motivated self-discipline and courage in this sensitive area. We owe Arlington's blood no less.

There is no area of life that is so subject to emotional manipulation as religion. People get emotional about eternal judgment. This is all the more reason that we must stop and think, to seek and find balance, in considering religious life in our nation. The believer must show and seek respect for the unbeliever, and the unbeliever for the believer.

All citizens have an obligation to retreat from tactics of public inflammation, and to advance upon the nobler path of reason, as the New Testament Book of Acts tells us the Apostle Paul did when he preached on Mars' hill in Athens. We need to reach a democracy in which individual choices are governed more thoroughly by thought than visceral reaction. Until we do, the false nutrition of each new day's emotionalism will continue to divert precious energy from more worthy causes, and it will continue to keep our great and diverse society off balance, thus providing a persisting insult to Arlington's blood and our own corporate dignity.

Americans should never stop working, never stop striving, and never stop fighting until there truly is liberty and justice for all. And liberty, justice and equality in America will not be fully realized so long as all able-bodied citizens are not provided a reasonable opportunity to attain at least a subsistence living standard through work.

History often repeats itself, showing that we are forgetful creatures. We seem bound to repeat the mistakes of the past after they were previously made and corrected. The irony of this situation is that new proponents of old mistakes often recycle error by believing that they are doing something new.

General Dwight D. Eisenhower's great record of military leadership allowed him to be elected to our presidency twice with strong public support. Some criticized him as a do-nothing President. However, his general policy of deliberate action is exactly what made him a great President. Doing "nothing," in reliance on the actions of the past, was the wisest economic course of action for his day.

General Eisenhower, a Republican, had the political support to have undone much of what had been done by the Democrats who preceded him, Franklin Roosevelt and Harry Truman. Yet, he did nothing of substance to undermine Roosevelt's progressive New Deal economic policies or Truman's military containment policy for communism. Why? Because General Eisenhower was wise enough not to try to fix what was not broken, and to stick with what worked. He understood that economic policies forcing monetary circulation and foreign policies that confronted aggression in a patient and consistent manner worked. And his era as President, from 1952 through 1960, remains an example of relative national peace and prosperity.

Thus, General Eisenhower was able to successfully do "nothing" because he was wise enough to recognize and sustain the successes of his predecessors. And his status as a military and political giant who refused to undermine past successes for partisan gain cemented those successful policies into place for the benefit of his nation's future.

Implementing economic errors that would cause another economic collapse will not destroy our democracy. We have survived several of them and will another if it comes. Wise voices will emerge again to lead us to reestablish what worked before. But we will lose greatly if we allow economic history to repeat in this way, for we will miss the opportunity to secure freedom from want. We will have to expend our energy to regain a plateau already conquered while still yearning for the land just over the mountain. Arlington's blood pleads that we march forward into that land in this generation.

It was also Franklin Roosevelt who said, "We have nothing to fear but fear itself." We can be free of the fears that harass us. We can participate wisely in foreign affairs without unduly placing the health or financial well being of our people or the sovereignty of our nation at risk. We can eliminate violence from our streets. And we can do so while maintaining a free and fair society. We have successfully met every challenge that has ever faced us. We need not fear that we will be unable to meet those before us today or tomorrow.

We can accept the mission for which the blood of those who went before us was spilled. Its voice still cries out from the past into the present imploring that we, this generation, make the decisions and do the work necessary to secure the blessings of liberty for 100 years after the dates of our deaths. There is no task nobler than working toward this goal, and there can be no greater honor than achieving it. Arlington's blood demands no less.

BIBLIOGRAPHY AND READING LIST

In keeping with the goal of rendering a project that, aside from personal experiences, any relatively informed citizen could have produced, I have tried to provide an easily readable offering of ideas and reasoning, not a reference work. The information for most of what I wrote has been garnered over the years just by reading the public information in the newspapers and government reports, such as from the census. But there are a few references that I have relied on for general information and background, and some that I just recommend as good works to read and learn from.

The Holy Bible (King James Version)

The United States Constitution

The Library of America (Viking Press compilation of foundational writings of American literature, biography and political thought)

Black's Law Dictionary

The Merck Manual (17th ed., 1999)

The Harper Encyclopedia of Military History (Dupuy and Dupuy, 4th ed., 1993)

On War (Carl von Clausewitz, 1832, translated and edited by Howard & Paret 1976, 1984)

Franklin D. Roosevelt, His Life and Times (edited by Graham & Wander, 1985)

John Adams (David McCullough, 2001)

Brains, Behavior and Robotics, ch. 12 (James S. Albus, 1981)

Common Sense (Thomas Paine, 1776)

War and Peace (Leo Tolstoy, 1869)

America: What Went Wrong? (Bartlett & Steele, 1992)

Debt and Taxes (Makin and Ornstein, 1994)

How Real is the Federal Deficit? (Eisner, 1986)

Dismantling America: the Rush to Deregulate (Tolchin, 1983)

Inquiry Into the Nature and Causes of the Wealth of Nations (Smith, 1776)

The Tyranny of the Status Quo (M. and R. Friedman, 1983 and 1984)

Macroeconomics (Mankiw, 5th ed., 2003)

The Flag Burning Case: Freedom of Speech When We Need it Most (Professor Arnold H. Loewy, 68 N.C.L.Rev.165, 1989)

Texas v. Johnson, 491 U.S. 397 (1989) (the flag burning case)

Terminiello v. Chicago, 337 U.S. 1 (1949) (protection for unpopular speech)

Red Lion Broadcasting Co. v. F.C.C., 395 U.S. 367 (1969) (upholding the fairness doctrine due to the "paramount" right of viewers and listeners with regard to broadcast messages)

McConnell v. F.E.C., ___ U.S. ___, 124 S.Ct. 619 (2003) (upholding parts of the McCain-Feingold campaign reform)

Buckley v. Valeo, 424 U.S. 1 (1976) (money as campaign speech)

Griswold v. Connecticut, 381 U.S. 479 (1965) (recognized right to privacy)

Roe v. Wade, 410 U.S. 113 (1973) (abortion within right to privacy)

Webster v. Reproductive Health Services, 492 U.S. 490 (1989) (modified Roe v. Wade)

Planned Parenthood v. Casey, ___ U.S. ___, 112 S.Ct. 2791 (1992) (reaffirmed Roe v. Wade)

Lawrence v. Texas, 539 U.S. 558 (2003) (homosexual relations within right to privacy, *reversing* Bowers v. Hardwick, 478 U.S. 186 (1986))

Elk Grove Unified School District v. Newdow, ___ U.S. ___ (dismissed for lack of standing 6/14/04) (the Pledge of Allegiance case)

0-595-32332-4